BONJOUR DIGGER

An Australian in France 1916

Herbert Scanlon

ETT IMPRINT
Exile Bay

Published by ETT Imprint, Exile Bay in 2025

Copyright in this edition © ETT Imprint 2025

Compiled by Tom Thompson

This book is copyright. Apart from any fair dealing for the purposes of private study, research, criticism or review, as permitted under the Copyright Act, no part may be reproduced by any process without written permission. Enquiries should be addressed to the publisher.

ETT IMPRINT
PO Box R1906

Royal Exchange NSW 1225
Australia

A Sydney-Paris Link publication
In memory of Jean-Paul Delamotte

ISBN 9781923205680 (paper)
ISBN 9781923205697 (ebook)

Cover by George Colville

Designed by Tom Thompson

Contents

Introduction   4
War Record of "Herbert Sanlon"   6
The Musical Bombardment   8
A War Baby   10
Little Mamzelle   13
Meeting Susette   16
Land of Memory   19
Chateau of the Dead   23
Memories of Little Mamzelle   26
Tell Them This   29
Mademoiselle Longun   32
Out on Night Patrol   42
My French Bride   55
The Limehouse Parade   58
M'sieur Giraud   61
A Shattered Romance   66
Nanette   70
A Tragedy of Love and War   75
The Game   89
The Unknown   101
Goodbye Susette   104
Take me - Give Me   107
The Eternal Silence   108
The Curse of the Brute   111
Goodbye   115
Rumination   117
Old Letter   119
Revisiting the Battlefield of France   120
Apres Le Guerre   121
Notes   122

INTRODUCTION

Herbert Scanlon was born in Korumburra, Victoria. Before he enlisted, his occupation was a farmer. At seventeen years of age Herbert Scanlon lied about his age when he came to enlist in the Australian Imperial Force in July 1915 as "Herbert Sanlon", as another Herbert Scanlon enlisted in his unit. In 1916 he arrived in France, which for many young Australians, was the biggest thing in their lives to date. He saw battles, billeting with French families and the reconstruction of French towns. In and out of auxiliary hospitals throughout his service, Scanlon was eventually honourably discharged in 1917 with a permanent disability and was sent home due to nephritis.

Unable to return to farming, he survived on a small military pension and began to write about his experiences during World War One. Scanlon's *Recollections of a Soldier's Life and Sundry Verse* was self-published in Ballarat in 1918 and his collection of fictional letters, *Gay Madamoiselles, Sly Digs and Wedding Bells* was published soon after. After the war Scanlon embarked on a career as a writer, eventually publishing some 17 short collections of short stories, poems and the occasional humorous episodes in 32 page booklets. While many of the stories were standard trench experience accounts, and involved memories of his life in England and Australia, it is the French stories that we will consider here, many written with great sensitivity and passion. Positive responses to these publications led Scanlon to continue publishing his series of small booklets of 'Digger Stories' which were sold door-to-door by struggling returned servicemen.

Scanlon's credentials as a returned serviceman were asserted in the opening pages of each booklet and the character of his salesmen was also stressed to protect against the negative reactions of a public wary of such endeavours. As his namesake Herbert Scanlon died a hero during the war, some reviewers felt that these stories were made up and perhaps his war experience was a fraud.

Scanlon's stories sit comfortably between their original stapled cardboard covers as examples of light romance, often set in the battlefields of France. The popularity of this genre and the persistence of his salesmen found a significant audience for the series. With titles printed in Sydney, Ballarat, Melbourne and Auckland, he was able to claim 100,000 readers for *Much in Little* by the mid-1920s. But, despite his success, Scanlon appears to have written nothing beyond this series. He died on 26 December 1936 as a result of injuries received in a fight, as sad an ending as the tragedies he witnessed in his beloved France.

HERBERT SANLON

Regimental number   2807
Place of birth   Korumburra, Victoria
True Name   SCANLON, Herbert
ReligionMethodist
Occupation   Farmer
Address 452 High Street, Preston, Victoria
Marital status   Single
Age at embarkation   21
Height 5' 5.5"
Weight 137 lbs
Next of kin : Brother, Frederick Sanlon, Emu Railway Station, Emu, Victoria
Previous military service Nil
Enlistment date 16 July 1915
Place of enlistment   Melbourne, Victoria
Rank on enlistment   Private
Unit name   22nd Battalion, 6th Reinforcement

AWM Embarkation Roll number 23/39/2 Embarkation details   Unit embarked from Melbourne, Victoria, on board HMAT A38 Ulysses on 27 October 1915
Rank from Nominal Roll   Private
Unit from Nominal Roll   59th Battalion
Fate   Returned to Australia 16 October 1916
Other details   War service: Egypt, Western Front
Allotted to and proceeded to join 57th Bn, 23 February 1916; joined Bn, Tel el Kebir, same day.
Admitted to 1st Australian General Hospital, 29 February 1916 (dental problem).
Transferred to 59th Bn, 15 March 1916.
Embarked Alexandria to join the British Expeditionary Force, 18 June 1916; disembarked Marseilles, France, 29 June 1916.

Admitted to 26th General Hospital, Etaples, 13 August 1916 (influenza), transferred to England, 22 August 1916 (nephritis), and admitted to 1st Southern General Hospital, Dudley Road; discharged from hospital, 16 October 1916 (nephritis, gun shot wound, slight).
Commenced return to Australia from Southampton on board HS *Karoola*, 16 October 1916; disembarked Melbourne, 2 December 1916; discharged (medically unfit), Melbourne, 12 February 1917.
Medals: British War Medal, Victory Medal

Declared by Statutory Declaration, 7 January 1919, that his true name was Herbert SCANLAN and that his true age at Attestation was 17 years 10 months.

Date of death   26 December 1936.

Edité par la Compagnie des CHEMINS de FER de l'EST

THE MUSICAL BOMBARDMENT

Perhaps it will be only the men who have suffered the agonies of a bombardment who will appreciate to the full this little story.

It was in 1916, on a section of front that was noted for its heavy bombardments. Behind our lines the guns were standing wheel for wheel; behind them again were guns and more guns. I do not know how many Fritzie had behind his lines, but he certainly could oblige us with as many shells as we favoured him with. When our guns began to shell his lines, he just retaliated in a manner that held our deepest respect.

For the men around the centre of the attraction "the front line" it was magnified hell. The day I am speaking of was a wet, depressing day. That is part and parcel of a Flanders winter. Our guns began to sing their melody in a desultory fashion, after the manner of its species.

A stray gun here would cough and be silent again. Another further up the line would pick up the melody where it had broken off and supply the missing note. Again, a roar from the centre of the line and the first bar would be completed. The big guns far away in the rear supplied the necessary bass. The opening stages of a bombardment are for all the world like a huge orchestra tuning their instrument in preparation for the combined effort that will follow.

We in the trenches catch the spirit of the moment, and move about our daily duties, cleaning rifles, etc., in a sprightly presto fashion. At last, after a lot of tuning, and as if obeying the conductor's baton, the first line of guns booms out the opening bars.

They get no applause - the dead Germans in the trench opposite are the bouquets they are striving for. But why dwell on such things? It was either they or we.

"Farewell beloved," so chain the sustaining pedal down tight and let us have it in volume; even if the melody is now becoming a little broken. There is always a trace of madness, gladness, and tragedy about a melody played with the loud pedal down. You feel it in a drawing room when the tinkling notes of the piano waft you away from the hum-drum of daily life to the wider, freer spaces where your spirit finds contentment in the realization of its dream.

What must it be to those men who hear the orchestra of the world - I may say the devil-playing lullabys with the loud pedal clamped down.

For truly it is a lullaby; it is the voice of Right crooning this world of ours from conflict and strife to an everlasting peace.

THE WAR BABY

It was a marvel to me how the old wrinkled Madam and her daughter stood it so well, seeing that their house was well within range of the Hun artillery. The stable at the rear of the house was practically demolished, all that remained of it was a few bare uprights. The house itself had not escaped, the walls were scarred with shrapnel bullets, the roof minus a few tiles, and all the windows broken. But these things were only secondary considerations to Madam and her daughter - it was their home. They still tended their little vegetable patch, still milked the ancient old cow, and, above all, tended to the needs of the troops that were billeted hereabouts. The fare was not sumptuous; honey, cake, beer and wine being the main commodities of the pantry. But Madam survived, and was always pleasant and cheerful. Her daughter was loved by all the Aussie boys. She was just a little thing, with a wistful, far-away look in her eyes. We gathered from the old lady that her husband was away up at Verdun with his regiment. We understood that dreamy look then - or thought we did. We missed her out of the estaminet one day. Madam seemed to be anxious and worried, and we could think of no reason for such a state of affairs. Madam would not have become excited if a shell landed fifty yards away. Her trust in our boys was absolutely sublime. Next day, the young Madam was still missing; and when we walked in Madam hurried out of an inner room; served us, and disappeared again. At last the truth dawned upon us - Madam was ill. We called the old lady and questioned her. She dropped her head and with a curious little smile said, "Oui, Monsieur." The smile was reassuring, but we forgot to mention this when we informed the doctor about it - our anxiety was too great. That night we went up to the front line on fatigue duty. Fritz was shelling the back areas heavily. We cursed him for his bad taste. Another night he would not be bothered doing it, but tonight, just because Madam was ill, he seemed to be taking a special interest in it. Our work finished for the night, we left the front line and proceeded to billets. We had a few hours' sleep and made our way around to our favorite rendezvqus. As we approached the place we could see little groups of men standing around. The blinds were drawn, the doors closed. So it was that sudden, was it? Fearing the worst, yet afraid to believe it, we questioned of one group: How is Madam this morning? I'm afraid she's very ill. The Doc. is with her now. We waited and conversed in hushed voices. When will we hear the verdict?" He has been in there half an hour now," one man exclaims petulantly. The least he could do is to let us know. There was a tragic stillness in the air that morning - the silence seemed. Intense after the recent bombardment.

At last we hear the rattle of the door handle; a few seconds and out stepped the doctor. He gazes around at the groups of men.

"What in the devil are you men doing here?" he questions in a voice that was meant to sound harsh, but was really cheerful, although a little broken. "Get back to your lines at once!"

"But, Sir," one man protested; "will she pull through alright?"

The doctor scratched his chin and considered for a moment or so. We gathered around him. At last he raised his head and laughed, a real hearty laugh.

"How did you fellows know?" he asked.

"Know what, Doctor?"

"That - er damn it all-that – er - it was that?"

"What is 'that,' Sir?"

"Oh, well, if you must know, it is a son, a fine big. boy, too. Do you men hear me? Get back to your lines at once."

Although it was no business of ours, we shook hands on the strength of it.

"Well, I'll be, jiggered," said one man, "Is that all it was..."

"Ain't that enough," answered a married man, becoming aggrieved.

We patronized Madam fifty per cent. better after that, just to give the kid a chance of having everything it needed. And then, when the kid was first shown to us by the proud young mother, Lord, we cheered and coo-eed it and her to the echo. We paid our homage in a hundred different ways. I saw a big strapping infantry man making his way to the estaminet a few days afterwards. His face wore a guilty look. His waist-belt was undone, and the front of his tunic was bulging out to an alarming extent. I was curious, so I said: "What's doing, Dig?"

He looked sheepish and moved from one foot to the other and said: "Oh, nothing. I'm just taking a stroll, Digger."

"Where to?" I questioned.

He had no need to answer me. From somewhere up around the region of his chest a spray of climbing roses slipped and dropped near his feet. Poor Digger. He was only human. He is dead now; but his memory is clearer to me for that little incident.

Another morning, Madam found two freshly plucked fowls on the door step. The same morning, one of our lads was fined £1 for being absent without leave. He took his punishment with a grin, and told me in a roundabout way that he walked close on two miles to raid that fowl house. But he reckoned it was worth while. So now you know all about our War Baby.

LITTLE MAMSELLE

Little Mademoiselle was a necessary part of our existence; she was such a winsome child. We had become so attached that every man took a personal interest in her. Her father had been a soldier, but was killed outside the village early in the war when she was only a wee toddler. But she had a dim recollection of the morning he said goodbye. She remembered how Mummy cried when Daddy left them. Daddy had often gone away before, but this time he had not come back.

Her childish imagination could not find any reason for this, and then every week Mummy went over to a little mound about two miles away, and sat there and cried.

All these things were mysteries to the child. Perhaps this is one reason why we took such an interest in her. She could speak very good English, in fact, more English than French. This was owing to her being with the British troops so much. We finished her education off by teaching her some of our own words. She would refer to anything that pleased her as "square dinkum," "straight." It was always a source of amusement to us to hear her say these words. She would always go to meet the boys who were coming out of the trenches for a few days' rest. She would hide by the roadside and spring out on us when we least expected to see her. It was generally when our packs and equipment were beginning to get extra heavy.

Her eager little face would scan the ranks for a special favourite. If we had left him behind she would say, "Naughty man. He has gone home without saying good-bye." We taught her to believe that they went home again.

She could not understand why every time we went up the road some of us never came back to see her. Little did she know how deep her artless words cut us, and little did she know she spoke a great truth. I myself am not ashamed to say that I often felt like blubbering when I heard her say-"Naughty man. He has gone home without saying good-bye."

Sometimes she would cry and count on her fingers, one, two, three, four, five, and say: "Will there be any more going home?"

Then when the wounded men were coming back from the trenches she would run up to them and say: "Did you fall over? Did it hurt?" I have seen men who were badly shattered, and knew their fate, answer: "Yes, deary, I did fall. But it is only a scratch, and it does not hurt one bit."

It would have been cruel to enlighten her. She would watch with.open-eyed wonder the long string of motor ambulances passing, and clap her hands in delight, and although it is a paradox, we loved her for it.

I remember well the night the Hun artillery bombarded the village. We were billeted in a loft, and had received orders to be ready to move off at a moment's notice. Shells were coming over fast and furious; Several had landed dangerously close. We were lying back on our packs when a terrific crash brought us hurriedly to our feet. Hardly had we recovered from the shock when another terrific explosion shook the building from end to end. Slates slithered down from the roof and crashed on to the paved yard below. "Down stairs, men!" an officer yelled. "Take what cover you can." We were not long obeying the order. Once outside we felt safer, and took to the open fields. Several of us took refuge in an old dug-out and passed the remainder of the night dozing and telling yarns.

At last daylight came, and with it the bombardment ceased. We made our way back to the billets. We were crossing one field, we noticed a group of men standing around a curiously hunched-up figure lying on the ground. We went over to see what the trouble was.

Lying on the ground was a soldier. Clasped in his
arms and underneath him, as if for protection, was a little figure in a nightdress. We removed our hats. It was our little Madamoiselle - dead.

So she had learned the truth at last - why some of us went home without saying goodbye. She still had the sweet little smile on her face, her arms were around her comrade's neck, her head snuggled into his shoulder.

"Well," said one man, breaking the silence; "it was instantaneous," and turned his head away. We covered their faces with a handkerchief, and with heavy hearts left them. The old road would have no pleasant surprises now ... the packs would not grow lighter. Nobody to miss the naughty, naughty men. One had taken her with him this time ...

We buried them that afternoon ... within sound of the guns ... together. It would have been sacrilege to part them. It was soldiers who held the fainting mother at the graveside. The old minister's voice was strangely mellow... We made no attempt to hide our tears. Poor little M'selle, it was hard that she should die like that. We raised a little cross over their heads and inscribed these words on it: "Our darling M'selle; her comrade and ours."

MEETING SUSETTE

Madam was all hurry and bustle and looked flushed with her preparations, as 1 stepped into the little front parlor. M'sieur must be weary; he would partake of some wine and then he must rest until the evening, for Madam had invited quite a lot of the village folk, and M'sieur would be very tired before he retired. So saying, Madam gave me a motherly kiss and departed into the kitchen to prepare the good things. The guests began to arrive: early, and I was greeted and kissed and fondled in an unaffected way by half the pretty girls of the village and their mamas and their papas, for was I not one of the brave Australians who fought fiercely, died with a smile, and loved and kissed so tenderly, and who would say nay if Mon Brave wanted to kiss tbe pretty red lips and claim the attention of the pretty girls, for was not he one who had defended them and suffered for them? There was no coyness; it was wholesome delight at having me with them again. They loved me, not for myself but for my countrymen, whom I at that moment represented. Would M'sieur condesend to kiss the little Mamzellc in the corner? She had been too young when the gallant Australians lived here, but now she had grown, and if M'sieur would greet her she would be glad. Who could resist the pleading old lady who asked me? Yes, M'sieur would gladly kiss the sweet Mamzelle. It was, indeed, a pleasant experience, for the girls of France are sweet, winsome creatures, with sparkling eyes and cherry-red lips, that were made for kissing, and in truth I found my self-imposed task an envious one to any but myself. Madam hovered in the background, flitting here and there, ridiculously excited and pleased, at the prospects of a pleasant evening. If M'sieur would care to dance she would clear the little room and play the piano for us. So we danced and sang and kissed in the joyous abandon of youth, forgetful of the past and conscious of the present. Faces were flushed, and eyes sparkled, for the good red wine of France warmed the blood and loosens the stiff joints. The music tinkled and sobbed a sweet refrain of love and life. Now and then Madam played a familiar army refrain, and to the rollicking tune we danced and danced. The old folk, to whom the tune brought back a flood of memory, sobbed quietly, for their sons were not here - they, too, were sleeping. and I in fancy danced not with sweet Mamzelles but with one of the dead gallants outside in the moonlight, for I had danced to the tune before when nights were long, and death hovered over us, and we did not know but the morrow would find our maimed bodies, or the useless clay that was us. Our dance then was the dance of uncertainty, and we danced with a false abandon. There memories will re-occur. But why dwell on the past? Tonight we live and mock at Death, tomorrow will claim it, own.

Madam ceased playing and prepared the table for supper. Madam's supper was her great concern. If the guests did not eat and eat, her evening would be spoiled. She had labored long and carefully over the dainty honey cakes and the lettuce salad, and had conjured up many delectable tit-bits from the deep, cool cellar - dainties that only French women can prepare correctly. M'sieur must have that, and he must try this, and the pretty girls and their mothers agreed that M'sieur Australian must have everything he desired, for was not his stay among them all too short, and before long he will be going back to his own home and perhaps he will never return. I must confess I hated the idea of leaving them - it was all so splendid, so very like the French people, to treat me like this. Soon the guests began to disperse, One Mamzelle to whom I had paid particular attention loitered behind, and, not being slow in matters of the heart, and sensing her design, I suggested that I should escort her home, to which suggestion she shyly consented. Will I ever forget that walk in the moonlight? – and how she somehow seemed to be part of this glorious country? The soft touch of her, the daintiness, the warm love welling in her eyes; surely she was Joan of Arc, so very effeminate and desirable, and yet the strong passion and loyalty of her! Is it any wonder the sons of France can fight, when they have such women to fight for? I kissed her tenderly at the door of the rose-covered cottage and bade her sleep sweetly.

LAND OF MEMORY

I trudged along the old road, now strangely quiet and peaceful. The hedge-rows were green and russet-brown, while here and there an early bloom gave promise of a glorious Spring. It was an ideal spot this bright day, a place for song and merriment, but ever at my heels trudged an army of men - Left-Right-Left - and unconsciously I hummed an old marching song, and felt the chafe of rifle and equipment. Reaching the crest of the hill, I looked down into the valley, and away beyond to the rolling plains of Flanders, green and peaceful looking in the bright sunlight. I shivered, for my mind bridged back over a span of years, and I heard the roll of cannon and the tramp of many men marching into battle. I marched with them again, up to the brink of hell and to the rim of eternity. Some passed across, some suffered the pangs of death and still lived, some there were whom the Gods of War loved and protected, or mocked, shielding them this once, and later flinging them into the awful void of darkness and silence Many I could call to mind who lay ahead sleeping peacefully now, with never wail of shell or screaming men to disturb them, faces to the enemy, with their duty well done.

Ahead of me, half-hidden by a fold in the earth, lies Etaples, the city of memory. Madam and the War Baby live down there: I would go and see them. I missed the signs of welcome that I naturally expected. I was not noticed. Well, tomorrow we would see what happened, for my uniform was my passport once, and so it would be again. The village I knew well - every street, ever house was impressed on my memory - and I soon found my way around to Madam's estaminet, in the Bois Boulevard.

A young French polui greeted me at the door, and on enquiring if Madam was in he ushered me inside the quaint parlour. Soon Madam herself appeared, and asked me what wine I preferred, for she had not recognized me, and thought I was a casual tourist.

On making my wants known, Madam recognised the voice. Her eyes brightened, and she told me in all her voluble French how M'sier was so welcome and madam so pleased. "And your mother?" I enquired, "Where is she?" "Ah, M'sieur," she said, speaking in a whisper,

"Madam, my mother, is gone. She, like the gallant 'Australiene,' has gone west. Iss it not what you say, Monsieur? The German shell, he kill her and our cow all at once." I sympathised with her, for I, too, had lost a dear one since those fateful days.

"The little one, Madam, where is he - the one we were so concerned about, our War Baby?" It was not until then did Madam fully realise that I was one of the little party billeted at her place in 1916, when the baby was born. She hugged me and kissed me and cried over me, and said, between her sobs, "My Australiene!" and kissed me some more. However, she soon recovered, and 1 gathered from her actions, and shrill, excited voice, that he was out on an errand and was a lamb! M'sieur was dispatched to the cellar for a bottle of the best vintage, and he went sullenly, for he had watched his wife kiss me and talk to me in a language he did not understand. and he was rebellious. Madam had been too excited to observe the formalities, and so it was not until he returned that I was introduced-and then the transformation, on finding out who I was. If anything, he was more profuse in his kissing, and more energetic, than Madam herself, and man-like departed to the cellar again, this time for champagne to toast my health. The champagne was a benediction. We cemented an eternal alliance over that glass; and to have the honor of cracking a bottle of the best in the cellar of a Frenchman is as lasting as the bond of blood. The boy returned, and I soon made myself acquainted with him. "You do not remember me, of course, do you?"

"No, M'sieur," Madam interrupted, "but he has been told of the Australians, and he picks flowers to put on the graves."

I told him of the fights we had taken part in, and could point out places that were written indelibly on my memory. I told him of the night he was born, and that a fierce bombardment was raging at the time. 1 impressed on him to always look after mother, for she was a brave woman to see it through.

We spent the evening around the fire, for the nights were still cold, and we talked of the days that were gone, and the old pals. Gone was the boasting and bravado, for her there is no humor in war - it is war, stark and grim. The dead live in this country, and the dead hear. Monsieur and I talked of the struggles and battles we had seen, he at Verdun, I on his own lands. Our hearts were at peace for the spirits of our dead - France and Australia - filled the little room and sipped and smoked with us. And lying peacefully on his bed was our War Baby, a strong link for the future alliance. I kissed him tenderly, for the good, true men who lay outside, underneath the bright stars, had fought and died to keep this little home intact for him, and had felt a little jealous at this intrusion in their billets, until they understood that the little Madam would soon be well again. I kissed him for them - their cold lips are closed in the seal of death. I kissed him for their own babies and unborn children, and on the faint breeze and out of the sweet-smelling night I heard a thousand voices say -"It is well."

CHATEAU OF THE DEAD

"Yes, M'sieur, that is the Chateau of La Mort, and you wonder why I tremble when I speak of it, for, Mon Dieu, if you will look, there is nothing dreadful in its appearance; but it is all so terrible. You who have seen the ebb and flow of battle, and death, swift and terrible, will understand, and before I finish you will know why my tears are ever ready to flow, why my eyes sparkle so - not with love, M'sieur, but with hate. There were worse things for us women of France than death, and the hand that you kissed, M'sieur, is stained with blood. I was my own avenger, and this hand - this little hand as you are pleased to call It - was strong, and my strength and spirit fierce. I was a good woman, a daughter of France, M'sieur, and it was a delight to see their death agonies. This mark on my breast was made by my hand. I did not die, although I prayed that it should be so. You wonder, M'sieur. Your embarrassment shows me you are surprised and shocked, but kiss me, Ami, before I told you my story, for I am not worthy of your love, and you should know why.

"My mother and I lived in the little cottage alongside the church - you will see it if you look between those trees yonder - and. we lived happily and peacefully, for I was the only child, and my wish was law to my devoted mother. My father was a business man in Paris, and when he died we came to live here. A modest income supplied all our needs, and life at that time was an eternal joy. We could not realise that sorrow would mar our joy in any way. I had been applauded by the great painting master of Europe and my picture was awarded the first prize in the Salon. This to a young girl, M'sieur, is a wonderful experience, for you understand it was my father's wish that I should become an artist of distinction, and so it was my one great ambition. Kiss me again, Ami, for I love to live again in those days. The sky was always blue, and life was sweet, and then - the affairs of the outer world scarcely troubled us here - we were a peaceful community, and it came as a great surprise to us to know France was at war. Even then we dismissed it from our minds, as something indefinite that would pass away overnight. But it was not to be, M'sieur. The rumbling of guns came nearer and disturbed our sleep. Little knots of wounded began to pass through the village, and, M'sieur, the armies of France began to retreat; and then we realised what war was, for we were in a direct line with the main enemy advance. My mother, in a urge of loyalty, caused the tricolor of France to be flown above our cottage. We thought the Germans would respect the women of France, but no, M'sieur, they came in hordes, and sneered and scoffed at our weakness, and insulted us. They - they came one night, M'sieur, and carried your little Susette away to La Mort, my mother was killed with a rifle butt when she tried to protect me - and I, M'sieur - you do not understand - I am but a girl, and M'sieur will not doubt me! They were sleeping one night, drunk with the wine of France. I was a woman of France, M'sieur; they had killed my mother. My soul was dead. Something inside of me cried for vengeance. Their helpless strength and gross features taunted me.

I killed them, and mocked them, even as their eyes glazed in death. I was not cowardly. This wound above my heart will show you I was not afraid; I desired it but it was not to be.

"That night the French advanced, and so I was saved. That is my story, M'sieur, and that is why the Chateau is called La Mort. You may scorn me, Ami, but my tears bring relief, and perhaps someday you will sympathise with me. Marry the woman of your heart, Ami, and tell her of Susette, and she . . . she will tell you."

For answer, I drew her gently to me, and while she sobbed on my breast the seed of love was born - her bright eye looked into mine and held me. "Susette," I said tenderly, sincerely, "I do not know your story - La Mort is but a dream."

Something inside of me cried for vengeance...

MEMORIES OF LITTLE MAMZELLE

Yes, I would put on my uniform to-day and go up to the front line and find the old, familiar landmarks. I told Madam of what I intended to do, and she was delighted. She would be off to the village if M'sieur had no objections, to get her vegetables, as they were very scarce yet, and the early buyer had a greater variety to choose from, and would M'sieur mind if tonight she gave a little party in honor of his return and invite a few Mamzelles, with bright eyes and red lips, to remind him that after all France was France, and Madam still remembered Monsieur's failing for the company of sweet Mamzelles. Yes, M'sieur was quite agreeable; in fact he thought it an excellent idea, looking at it in whichever light you please. Madam left me, flushed and roguish looking. I proceeded with my dressing, and must say I did credit to my native land, for I was trimly built and my uniform was nicely pressed.

Lighting a cigarette, I strolled outside and soon became the centre of an admiring group oi villagers, who greeted me with delighted surprise, for, as I expected, my uniform was my passport to their hearts, and they who saw me told others that an Australian soldier had arrived in the village. I greeted many whom I remembered; the old cure, with his snow-white hair, blessed me, and haggard old dames, with scanty hair and cold, fearless eyes, warmed to me, for we Australians could cut more wood and draw more water in one hour than they could from dawn to sunset, and it takes an old lady to remember a little kindness like that. I stepped out bravely and with a feeling of great pride. They had made me their king for the time being, not for myself but for the country my uniform represented. I was soon in the open fields. The ground is still serried and pock- marked with shell holes, and the reserve trenches were overgrown with weeds and tall, lank grass. So I went on to the second and first line of resistance, pausing now and again to let my mind roam at will over many memories. That dug-out to my left was my home for three desperate days. There, alongside of it, is a grave. I know it well. It was I who scooped the cavity with my entrenching tool, and sent a prayer to Heaven for the soul of the lad who went before. I went across No-Man's-Land, over and beyond the once German trenches. Once we fought for months to gain this strip of country; now it is useless. A strange, sinister silence broods over it, an uncanny feeling grips you. You long for the sound of cannon again, not because you like it, but because the silence does not seem real, and by the noise we knew it. Retracing my steps, I went to a field a little way from the road, across a small creek, and on until I discovered the object of my search - a little cross with these words on it: "Our Darling Mamzelle, Her Comrade and Ours."

  I tended the grave carefully. A big, rough digger lay beneath, and in his dead arms he clasped a little figure in a pitiful little white night-dress, stained with their blood. You remember how they died - he tried to save her and they were both struck down; and so we found them and buried them. No, it does not seem so long ago since she called the dead men the naughty men, for leaving her without saying good-bye, and laughed with delight to see a sorely-wounded man make faces for her to laugh at. Dear little soul, I thought, as I plucked a weed from the head of the grave, what unborn knowledge and sorrow you carried into that mound of earth. And the big soldier lying there with her, clasping her for protection: so he would take her across the valley of the shadow to her home. Dear little Mamzelle, what joy and comfort you brought the weary soldier, who thousands of miles away from bis own land, stroked and kissed your pretty hair and baby face, and so you lie with the sleeping men, in the land of sorrow and beauty, where mothers' hearts and thoughts arc hovering over your grave today, for France is not a strange country to them, but a memory of good sons and brave gentlemen, and so we leave you sleep, little girl, in your comrade's arms. I bared my head to the memory of the grief-stricken mother who mourned with us that day -they were buried- and to the rough soldiers who sobbed unashamed, as the earth was heaped upon them. In fancy I kissed her baby lips again, and told her not to be afraid - we were there to stop the Germans! All things must end, and so I left them, sadly, and with many a backward glance, for it is one thing to see a soldier die on the field of battle and another to see a sweet child mangled by enemy guns.

I passed many familiar places on my way home to the village, and dotted here and there are the little crosses that mark the dead, for this is the land of dead men and wistful dreams, and many of those crosses reared their heads not above soldiers, but dear pals of mine. My heart was heavy and my spirit dulled. I felt a wistful desire to be with them; voices seemed to call me and greet me. The sweet-smelling countryside and the bright sun spoke of peace, quiet, restful peace. I communed with their spirits and wended my way home, and, tramp, tramp, tramp, the phantom army followed me, all in perfect unison, for my heart rested with them, and I - I understood.

TELL THEM THIS

Away back in 1916, while billeted in a tiny village in France, I made the acquaintance of a young French student, who was not then of military age, and therefor ineligible for service with the Colours. A true patriot, with a keen sense of appreciation for the men of other countries who had covered thousands of miles to come to fight for his country - he soon made himself popular with the rank and file. I personally struck up a great friendship with him, no doubt owing to our mutual regard for literature.

I will never forget the morning we marched away from the village on our way up to the front, and often on a wet, cold evening, in fancy, I see him standing in the cold dawn, erect, but with trembling lips and unashamed tears coursing down his checks.

"Bon Sonte," he called, "I will write, Monsieur." "Good luck," I called back, "I will write, Jean."

Poor Jean, he has been dead these many years, killed at Verdun, where the pent-up fury of war spewed out its wrath of hot metal and death on the gallant defenders. Poor Jean! Little did he know, or will he ever know, that the letter he wrote to me one day in far away 1916 would be published many years afterwards, or that his letter would see so much of the horror or the human side of war, or that I would not see the letter or its contents for nearly fourteen years afterwards.

The letter arrived in my mail some time ago, and the covering envelope bore a German post mark from the City of Strasbourg. In it the writer - an ex-German soldier - told how he had picked the letter up on the battlefield and had kept it for a souvenir, and after a lapse of fourteen years had discovered it again, and when speaking one day to an Englishman it had been suggested to forward the letter on, in the hope of finding the addressee. It must be admitted that the letter has a strange history. And for this reason, and the fact of his great admiration for the Australian troops, I intend to publish it, as the letter to me is a poignant reminder of poor, brave Jean, the thoughtful young student, standing on the threshold of life and the brink of eternity. The translation of the letter is as follows:

July, 1916.

Dear Monsieur Scanlon,

True to my promise, I write you these lines, trusting and praying to God that it will find you well, contented as it is possible to be, and victorious.

I pray every night that the Boche will give before you and that this terrible slaughter will all soon be done with.

Things for the village here are much the same; the Mayor's youngest son was killed two days ago; he and his good wife are prostrated with grief. That makes three in the family - there are no more boys to go, but I do believe their sister Eloise - the very pretty one - would go if it were possible.

Yesterday the list of the killed was posted up at the hall, and the names included Francis Garden, Jules Lecomte, Pierre Laung, and Galde Bouchier - you know their sisters and mothers, and I will convey your sympathy.

Mamam is very worried about the war, and is afraid that I will have to go with my comrades, but, if that were so, I would be glad, for it hurts me to read the names of my friends in the lists, and know I cannot go for at least another year.

Our rations are very low. I thought to be able to send you some cheese in this parcel, but poor old Susan has gone dry for the want of fodder.

The parcel was the best Mamam and I could do and Nanette has knitted you a pair of mittens. She prays that God will keep your heart and hands warm, and she bids me tell you that her prayers are with you.

Three days ago we had some more troops in the village from New Zealand; it warmed our hearts to see them. Such fine big men, with on her hands. I turned to protest with her, but she anticipated me and said "Come!" I followed, with bowed head and aching heart, praying the while to my God to help her and me. She led me on, into the grounds of La Mort, and pointed out a tiny mound.

With heaving bosom and clenched hands, she confronted me. "Ami," she said, and her voice was broken, "that - and she pointed to the grave - was mine and theirs.... My baby," she sobbed - Ami, forget me -"kiss me once more, and then you must go, for ever."

Out of the sweetness of her kiss hate and sorrow were born; it was a kiss of dry ashes. A hatred for the great wrong sustained, consumed me; sorrow because I could not share it with her. I was willing, but her natural refinement was a barrier between us, and we parted in the grounds of La Mort for ever, I to a life of loneliness, she to the same.

Thousands of miles separate us now. but God gave dreams and God has helped me to believe La Mort was but a dream.

MADEMOISELLE LONGUN

The three soldiers lay stretched out on the cellar floor of the ruined estaminet. They were dead, in one sense, and around them on the floor, lay the empties that spoke eloquently of their not unpleasant manner of passing - *vin blong* - or for the benefit of the unknowing - the cheap wine of France.

Now this was not a deliberate carouse; it just simply happened - as things will happen in wartime, and it came about in this way.

Yesterday, the battalion had advanced through the enemy front for five miles and had succeeded in occupying this French village which was deserted by its citizens.

For two days the fighting had continued, and the battalion had held on in the face of a hell of a bombardment of shell and aerial fire. They had no food - having exhausted their battle rations - and the rest of the brigade had not kept up with them owing to a reverse on the left flank. At nightfall a messenger was despatched back over the canal to try and get in touch with the rest of the army, and the shell fire having died down, the men were told to forage through the village and find what they could eat.

Private Longun, when this command became known to him, made his way along the shallow trench that had hastily been thrown up, to his two pals Nugget Smith and Darkie White, and whispered into their ears: "Come along with me, my powers of navigation and imagination. have given me an idea - get your brains out of them moth balls and lavender and I'll lead."

"Don't wake up the mob, Nugget," he hissed, as that worthy asked what for, "Just slip along after me down that trench leading to the canal, and use your brains."

Knowing from experience the value of Longun's powers of perception on foraging expeditions, the three men followed the leader and tried to look disinterested in each other. He led the way along the communication trench, and when out of sight and hearing, he slid over the top of the trench, and bidding them keep low, headed for the outskirts of the village.

They followed him to a deserted house, that loomed out stark and dismal in the night air - the door swung idly on its hinges, mutely testifying to the hurried departure of the owners - and once inside he escorted them down into the cellar.

It was a cosy sort of cellar, and several hogsheads stood in one corner in almost appealing attitudes. They were empty, but from a cupboard along a dark passage that ran towards the rear of the house, Longun brought three bottles of Vin.

"Gee!" murmured Nugget piously, as a bottle was handed to him, "if he isn't Santa Claus in disguise - where did you get it from?"

"Is there any more of it? or is there any more round about?"

"Believe me," said Longun, indignant at the casual way in which his great find was being taken, "if it wasn't for me, you two jokers would never have have got a spot. You're dead from the heels up."

The corks popped and the wine went on its destined way. More followed, and the world grew darker outside. Darkie found a two-inch butt of candle in his pocket and inserted it in the neck of an empty bottle and struck a match.

They bung strips of sacking over the two windows in case someone came mooning around, and all was cosy, and it became cozier.

It was a glorious party while it lasted, but the trouble was it did not last long enough - wine has a way with it on an empty stomach, and the three comrades had not tasted food since the morning.

At last Nugget staggered to his feet to lead the way back to the regiment; he found his legs strangely unwilling; in fact, he subsided on the floor again, and in spite of his hard won reputation as a human sink - he laid down.

Even Longun swayed majestically and flopped into a little heap.

"I ain't going home," tall Darkie hiccoughed. 'I'm gonna shleep here."

"Too right," groaned Nugget. "T 'ell with the war."

Nugget crawled to the candle and snuffed it. "Soldiers," he sneered, "never said your prayers 'fore you went shleep - shame" - and his voice trailed away.

A lovely war - in spots.

In spite of the sacking over the windows the place had grown brighter. It's hard to keep daylight out, even in a cellar.

Someone sat up sharply. "Gee up Nugget, Darkie. Time we got back to the company."

"Oh, me head," quavered Nugget, holding his temples between his hands. "Where's some water?"

"There's some more *Vin*. Want a hair out of the dog that bit you?"

"Oh, shut up," groaned Nugget. 'I'm real bad."

"Hope they got some rations today" grumbled Darkie. "I'm empty as a barrel."

"Yes,' sneered Longun. "Even around the ears; Wait till I pull that sacking away so's we can see our way out." Daylight streamed into the cellar. Suddenly Longun let out a gasp and gazed out the window. Strike him pink if he wasn't still drunk, for there along the sunken road not five hundred yards distant, a platoon of grey uniformed soldiers were marching toward the canal. German soldiers, and they seemed to be quite at home.

He called his two mates to the window, and when they saw, their jaws dropped and the effects of the *vin* slipped from them suddenly.

"Cripes," said Longun, "they've either driven our chaps back, or we got orders to retire. We must have retired, or we would have heard the fighting."

"You - you wouldn'ta heard the crack of doom or Gabriel sounding the rally," Nugget observed bitterly. "Hell of a mess you've got us in, jest because you two stiffs can't hold their liquor."

"Shut up will you," groaned Darkie. "You're not the only one who wanes a drink of water." Then at the thought of water he turned on Longun. "You an' your navigation, an' your nose for liquor - it'll get you into trouble yet. All the trouble Nugget an' I have got into in this war was through you."

Longun felt miserable. The parson said "Wine was a mocker." He felt sure that parson was right, and besides, he felt he would die if he did not get some water - the banter of his pals was nothing - either of the trio would fight a dozen for each other, but what was to be done?

"Oh, go and drown yourself," he said viciously. "My party, my *vin*, now your rousing."

"I'm going upstairs," he said after a few moments. "There must be some water or grub, an' if we can get that we can hide here. Keep an eye on the window and if you see any of them Huns turn this way yell out to me. See?"

He disappeared up the stairs. They could hear him moving cautiously about the house as they kept their eyes glued to the window, but they had little hope of him finding anything to eat, for the place had been pretty well wrecked in yesterday's shelling.

Ten minutes later he returned.

"Any water up there?" Nugget demanded.

"No, but there's a well out in the garden."

"Any tucker?"

"A dead tom cat. He's quite fresh - feel hungry Dark?" he said pointedly.

"What's that you got, Longun," Darkie asked, pointing to a bundle of old clothes that hung over his arm.

"Women's clothes," he grinned. "Found 'em in a room upstairs. Only thing left in the place. Some Jane, too. All scented nice."

"Oh, mammie, boy," sneered Darkie, "come kiss papa. Did you bring the hand basin an' the clean linen - it's your party Aunty."

Then an idea dawned on him, and his eyes narrowed.

"Longun," he drawled, "you tried to impersonate a general up at Amiens once, and made a mess of it, but Nugget and me'll give you a chance to make good. We'll dress you up as a French dame, an' send him out for some water," he said turning to Nugget. "Get me, Nug?"

Longun gazed at them dumbfounded. "Like hell, you are," he shouted. "What do you take me for. What do you think I am? - a -" and he struck a belligerent attitude.

"Listen, now, Longun," Darkic said soothingly. "We've got to eat and drink. Them clothes are too small for us - they'd just suit you. "No, no," he remonstrated, as Longun advanced on him again. "I don't mean that; but you've got a poor figure for a man, an' you'd make a fine woman. You know, just kidding like a fancy dress ball. Get me? Then you can go out an -"

"Yes, I can go out, an' so can pigs fly," Longun burst out. "Look at my face; four days' growth of whiskers - that wouldn't fool a Hun, would it?"

Darkie's face fell. He had not thought of that. "Well," he said gloomily, "life in a German prison camp can't be worse than starving to death."

"Well," Nugget groaned, "if we've got to surrender, let's do it quick. I'll die if I don't get a drink. I feel like dying anyway."

Longun looked at his two pals. They were his mates. He'd got them into this mess. It was up to him to get them out. "Listen, you chaps," he said at length. "I'll do it?"

"You will?" Nugget brightened up considerably as a gleam of hope broke in on his sorrow.

"Yes! Tonight, as soon as it's dusk. I'll get into these togs and have a moon around - will that stop your grousing?"

"What about goin' out to the well now and getting some water," wailed Nugget. "Honest to goodness, I feel something awful."

"Listen," said Longun exasperated, "if I've got to be the goat, I'm not goating until the goating's good. I don't want to be no fat Hun's sweetheart - see? And in the meantime I'm going to have a drink, and if you don't like it do the other thing, and that means you, Nugget."

More wine was produced, and the trio drank deeply, but were cautioned by Longun not to take much or they would be going out and challenging the whole Hun army alone.

"My word, it's better than water," gasped Nugget as the fiery liquid warmed his interior. "I wasn't going crook, Longun. I was only barracking you."

Darkie agreed that it could not make him feel any worse than what he was.

The long foodless day wore on to its close. They discussed the relative merits of bully beef and the tom cat upstairs, and decided unanimously for bully beef, and pleasant conversation and *vin* helped while the day away.

The shadows began to lengthen in the war torn world outside, and Longun rose to his feet, yawned, and said:

"Well, I'll get frocked up for the party now. Hand them *crepe de chines* what's-a-names over. Better put 'em on. If I strike an amorous Hun, it'll give me a better chance," which observation brought forth irreverent sniggers from his companions, "An' I'll take my bayonet, in case he gets too fresh - it's no use taking a bomb; kick up too much noise," he added.

Longun lee himself out at the back of the house. A quarter of a mile away he could see a line of trenches that the enemy had been digging all day.

In the fading light he did not look unlike a French peasant woman, except when he climbed a fence, and the shawl that he wore over his head hid all his hair; but he had no desire to test his disguise unless absolutely forced co.

He made his way cautiously toward the village, taking advantage of all available cover, now resting behind some shrubs, then along a garden wall, and so along a narrow alley way between two houses, which led into the village square.

He heard voices here and pressed close into the wall in a convenient shadow. The voices droned on and he listened intently. He took a step forward, and then another.

Silhouetted against a light coming from a trench. kitchen, two Huns stood talking, and Longun noted by the distinguishing badges that one was a sergeant and the other an officer.

Directly, the officer moved away and the sergeant saluted briskly, swung around and walked in the direction in which Longun stood insecurely hidden.

Flight would have meant disaster, although this was Longun's first thought. That he would be detected was certainty, so he decided to brazen it out, and stepping out of the protecting shadow, tripped along about forty paces ahead of the sergeant and in the direction of the open fields away from the town.

He head the German sergeant's low whistle of surprise, and heard him pause for a second as if undecided what to do - and then he heard him quicken his steps.

Longun's heart beat a rapid pat-a-pat, and surely no young lady was ever so overcome with mingled emotions.

He tripped along as demurely as possible, always to the open fields and the less frequented spots, it being his idea to get the sergeant away to the open and then deal with him the best way he could.

He hoped devoutly that the sergeant's haversack would be well filled with sausage and bread.

A small copse loomed up out of the darkness ahead, and Longun slowed down. The very place for a dirty deed, he thought grimly, and he felt for his bayonet, which was hidden in the folds of his dress.

"Sprechen sie deutsch," the German said pleasantly.

Longun knew no German, and mighty little French, but he realised that the sergeant's intentions were eager rather than honourable.

"No compree," said Longun in a falsetto voice.

The German seemed disappointed, but tried to keep up the conversation in French. "Tres bon, see war Madamoiselle."

Not to be outdone, yet wondering what was going to happen when he ran out of his French, Longun replied: "San Ferry Ann."

The big German gave a grunt of satisfaction as Longun stepped behind the bush.

For a split second he thought of grabbing the Hun's revolver, but the thought was a split second too late, for the big sergeant caught Longun by the arm and gave it a gentle squeeze: "Bien! Frity," declared Tres Bon Madamoiselle.

"You quitta vous; nap poo, lumpa tripe," said Longun floundering horribly.

"Pardon, Mamyelle," exclaimed the Hun in a puzzled way. "No comprie French," and he sidled towards the apparently very agreeable fraulein. Madam sidled away.

He jammed his revolver well into his pocket and reached out with his two free hands, but Madam moved a thought quicker than the Hun, and as Longun grabbed for his bayonet the German bawled "Gott im Himmel," for Longun's veil had slipped from his head, and he saw the whiskers on his beloved.

Longun's bayonet flashed in one short, wicked, little jab and the Hun rolled over with a little moan. "That'll teach you to be true to the missus," Longun snorted grimly. "Us girls have to look after ourselves."

He ransacked the prostrate Hun's haversack and felt pleased that he was a big Hun for the ration department held two sausages and a lump of bread, that looked good to a hungry man.

He made his way back to the deserted house, and let himself in cautiously.

"Any luck," two voices asked in unison, when he had shut the door.

Longun laid his haul out on top of a barrel. "Have a look at this," he chuckled gleefully.

"Good boy, Longun," Nugget said reverently. "Darkie, come an' see what the nice kind lady has brought us. How did you do it?"

Longun told them briefly. They ate the bread and sausages sparingly for they knew that they may have to stop in the cellar for another day or so, or until such time as the brigade attacked again. They were in comparative safety here and decided to stay.

"Well," said Longun, after the repast was finished. "I'm going to get out of this female stuff. It ain't right that I should lay me down to sleep with you chaps, with them on. That big square head gave me a terrible fright. He was very loving." Then as an after thought he added, "If you two mugs tell any of the batt. about this there'll be a devil of a row between us - they'll call me Sis."

The night hours dragged on. While two slept, one kept watch. It was on Nugget's watch at 3.30 in the morning that a burst of machine gun fire shattered the silence.

Then bang, crash, bang, the big guns took up the music and made the night a medley of noise.

Nugget hurriedly woke his companions. "The Batt. is attacking," he yelled above the din. "Barricade those doors in case any Fritzies dive in here for shelter. Get them Mill's bombs, Darkie, and blow up the first Hun that comes this way."

Nugget and Longun took up positions at the window that faced the Hun lines, with eyes glued to their rifle sights.

In a few minutes a big lanky Hun loomed up out of the mists. Longun's rifle spoke, and the Hun sagged to his knees. "Got him," he said grimly.

The next ten minutes was spent in taking pot shots at the retreating Huns, until there were so many that the trio decided that it would be advisable to withhold their fire in case they gave their hiding place away.

"The boys are driving Fritz back, I imagine," said Longun. "They ought to be here any minute now." He broke off his sentence to take a pot shot at a big Fritz who seemed intent on making the house his temporary abode.

Then above the din they heard a cheer. A good British cheer, and they knew that the first German lines had been captured.

"Here they come," yelled Darkie from his vantage point, "at the trot, too. They've got the square head streaking for Berlin. Come on you stiffs," he yelled excitedly. "We'll be in this."

"You'll keep in here, you mug," bawled Longun, "or you'll get one of our bullets. Wait till the first wave passes. If they see your ugly dial they'll fire. You look like a square head."

A sergeant with a team of bombers rushed up to the deserted house and gave orders to search for cellars or dug outs. "If there's anyone in there," he yelled, "give 'em a bomb."

"Hold your horses," screamed Longun. "We're here, Sarg. Three of us.

"Well, up with your hands," the sergeant ordered, unable to see the owner of the voice, "and come out here. No funny business, or you'll not see daylight - come on!"

The three comrades trooped out of the cellar with their hands stretched above their heads.

"Spies," the sergeant said grimly, prodding them wickedly with his revolver, whereon Longun did the best piece of female impersonation he had done yet - and fainted.

The troops took the village that night. An officer came to see the three pals, who were safely imprisoned in the barbwire barricade. He questioned them, inspected them, and lectured them, and then told them they were lucky. "Now get back to your battalion. They are on the right of us," he directed. "Beat it!"

Five minutes later they were plodding their way through the ruined town.

Longun broke the silence. "Listen, you blokes," he said hopefully, "there's still six bottles left in the cellar. What say we lift 'em to cheer us on our homeward way."

The other two stopped dead.

"Well of all the -" Darkie ejaculated.

"You overgrown son of a gun," said Nugget. "If I ever hear you mention *vin blong* again this side of peace," and he eyed Longun with the severity of a stern parent, "I'll make a human sacrifice of you."

OUT ON NIGHT PATROL

Introduction

A Patrol - or listening post - was a very essential part of trench warfare, in that it helped us to gain much valuable information regarding the enemy's activities, the quality of the men opposed to us on our particular sector, and a rough idea of his machine-gun and trench-mortar positions. It was the duty of men selected for the dangerous and trying work to approach as close to the enemy trenches as possible, under cover of night, and watch and listen for any unusual movement that may be the preliminary to a raid, a gas attack, or a general assault.

Fighting was not to be indulged in, unless the enemy discovered the listeners and tried to drive them off - silence and nerve were the essential make-up of the ideal patrol.

The weapons used were generally bombs, revolvers, waddies (or in the vernacular) potato mashers, and daggers, and these were used at close quarters when the necessity arose.

It was usual to smear the face with burnt cork or mud, and in one epic instance on the Somme, in the winter of 1916 - when snow covered the countryside - a patrol went out in ladies' nightdresses and lingerie - the whiteness of the linen helping to hide them from the sharp eyes of the German sniper. Needless to say, many of the patrol went to their death in those white, simple garments.

The Author himself had an experience in July 1916, which, although very trying, was an experience never to be forgotten.

We had approached to within fifty yards of the German front line when out of the darkness we' saw eight Germans worming their way along in the mud - we lay very still, hardly daring to breathe, but they veered to our left and passed within ten yards of us - they were on their way to "listen in" at our trenches, we were on our way to theirs for a similar purpose - I do not know if they had seen us - if they did it was by mutual consent that we did not fire; for if we or they had done so, both parties would have been caught between two fires, as both friend and foe are touchy on the trigger at night time, and it takes little commotion to cause an "all in" fight. Weapons are carried only in the case of. emergency.

It is well to understand this before reading the following story, or many good soldiers will ridicule my portrayal of what they may regard as a raid - which is essentially a fighting party.

The story is not a pretty one - but war is war - and I have lifted aside the veil off one of the little episodes of the Great War, little episodes that took a great toll of lives, that account for many missing men - as it was necessary to remove all identification discs, letters, etc., that would help the enemy to arrive at a definite conclusion as to the Division and troops opposed to him.

OUT ON NIGHT PATROL

The shattered village of Merlincourt stretched its tumbled ruins along the top of the low ridge that marked the Allies lines.

To the right a shell tom wood marked the apex of the German trenches, which sheltered a nest of machine guns, and from which every few minutes came the sharp stacatto bark of a heavy maxim - rat-a-tat-a-tat - and the hissing steel-nosed bullets kicked up spurts of dust or chipped bits of stone and masonry from the walls that still stood as though in defiance of war.

The put-a-put of a one-lunged motor cycle broke a temporary silence as it bounced and skidded over the crazy sunken road that led into the village, and at the sound of it, grim jawed Boche gunners squinted over their sights and fired in the direction of the noise.

A muddy dispatch driver flung himself off his machine and dived for cover into the nearest dug-out. "Hey! Who's in charge of this place?" he yelled into the darkened interior; "where can I find him?"

"You'll find him in pieces if you don't stop that yelling, you dope. Fritz is only forty yards away, and he may get excited. He's on the other side of the street five shell holes up, and crawl on your knees if you want to see home and beauty. You've kicked up enough row to wake the German Army," the invisible voice complained.

But the dispatch rider had already left and was half way across the street, crouching low and taking advantage of all available cover.

Feeling his way cautiously in the darkness, he at last came to Headquarters, Shell Hole No. 5, and asked for the officer commanding.

"Here!" a voice whispered, "don't make a noise." The runner slid over the lip of the hole. "Lieutenant Jones, Sir?" he asked. "Message for you, Sir. This is A Company, isn't it?"

"Yes, that's me," a voice answered back. "Captain Smith went west last night. A shell got him. I'm in command."

He fumbled for the proffered note, and carefully shielding the rays of his torch with his helmet, read it through quickly, then again slowly and deliberately.

"Hell!" he said, addressing the mud-bespattered rider. "What fool sent this. Is it from Headquarters?"

"Yes, Sir, I know nothing about it. My orders are to stay here until you send your answer."

Lieutenant Jones clicked his tongue. "Oh, alright, make yourself at home, but don't be noisy about it. That old machine of yours might have brought on another shelling," he grumbled. And then as an apology, "here, have a nip out of this flask - go steady, that's all we've got - might want it before the night's out. I'll get down the street to a dug-out and get this answer," he whispered back as he crawled silently out of the muddy hole.

Finding a suitable dug-out he disturbed the slumbering sergeant. "Chock up those holes," he commanded, "and pull the hessian over the door - got to have a light - some brass hat fool wants to know how many men we can release from duty."

"But, Sir," the sergeant volunteered, "we have not half enough. You're the only officer left. We lost fifteen men today, and as it is we are only quarter strength. Sergeant Morgan, Corporal Brown and Hall went west today and twelve men," and, he muttered darkly, "we have to go through tonight."

"Yes, I know - I know," Lieutenant Jones said wearily, "but I'll have to do something - that is not a suitable explanation for the Brass Hats. If they want men they'll get 'em, and if not they'll take 'em," and he laid his automatic on the up-turned box.

The Sergeant fingered his captured Luger lovingy, and with a wicked smirk, he gave it as his opinion that Headquarters was the enemy, not the men in the opposing trenches.

Lieutenant Jones favoured him with a warning stare. "No time for that, Sergeant. It's H.Q.'s war as well as ours, and if they don't understand - well, it's because they are not here. Some of them would not know a Frog from a Hun."

Before the Sergeant could frame a suitable remark, a figure slipped through the dug-out door, and a Corporal clicked to attention. "The telephone is open again, Sir. The line's clear and they are calling Captain Smith - told 'em Captain Smith got killed yesterday, Sir - and they want to speak to second in command."

The Lieutenant swore inwardly. "I sent two runners to report that. Could not have got through," he muttered. "All right, Corporal, coming now; keep the line open."

In No. I dug-out the field telephone buzzed, subdued but insistently. "Hello! Colonel Helper here. Is that the officer in command." "Yes, Sir, Lieutenant Jones here. What is that, Sir? A patrol tonight to be led in person by an officer? But listen, I'm the only officer--"

He stopped suddenly, and almost threw the earpieces at the Corporal.

"Gone again - and God knows when they will get it going again. A patrol inside the German lines tonight, and an officer has got to lead it. I tried to tell the fools that I'm the only officer around here, but the line broke before I got a chance. Who will I leave in command, anyway? That fool runner they sent along - he woke every Hun on the front.

"The chances are that they will get no reply to that fool question of theirs. I'm not labouring under any illusions as to what chance the patrol has of coming back. That wood is lousy with Boches - about ten to every one of us, I'm guessing. and they want information in a hurry." The Lieutenant spat disgustingly.

"Sergeant, I guess you will have to take charge. What time is it? Nine o'clock! I thought it was getting late. I wish you good luck if anything happens in this place. If I stay here I'll get hell, and if I go and get back I'll probably get the same for leaving my command. Oh well. go out and collect a Corporal and five other men, and have them here in a half-hour; and don't forget to tell the others that there is a patrol out tonight. Don't want to get shot by our own."

"Yes, Sir." The Sergeant saluted and slipped out into the night.

Clouds were blowing up from the west, to shut off even the faint light of the stars. The Lieutenant peered out. "Storm, I guess. Hope it doesn't catch us on patrol. The line still dead, Corporal?"

"Yes, Sir; as dead as Methusaleh. Hope Fritz does not attack, or H.Q. would not know of it."

"Oh well." Lieutenant Smith shrugged, "It's me for it. Patrol it is, and if I don't see you in Potsdam, I'll see you in Hades."

The hessian over the entrance swished softly, and the Sergeant stepped in. "The men are outside, Sir," be said, saluting.

"Bring them in, Sergeant!"

Lieutenant Smith viewed his patrol "All right," he said. "They'll do." Then addressing: the men in a louder voice:

"Now, you men, you know what we are here for. We are going out on patrol, to try and get information as to what Fritz is doing. See?

"No noise, and no talking. Get the idea? I don't want any firing without my orders. We're not going out to fight, we're going out to be as inconspicuous as possible."

"Everybody got wire-cutters, grenades and pistols ready? Take a potato masher each and leave all badges and identification discs behind, and if any of us are captured keep silent to all questions asked you. Rub some mud on your hands and face when we get outside - we will be less easily seen.

"All ready, now? I will lead. Corporal Fraser will bring up the rear, and do nothing without my orders. Sergeant, you are in charge of Merlincourt, and I wish you luck"; and the slim, boyish Lieutenant came to the salute.

"Thank you, Sir, and good luck to you, Sir," the Sergeant muttered grimly, although in a strangely subdued voice.

They left Merlin-Court through a short, deserted trench leading down the slope towards the German positions.

Our of this, they wormed their way through mud and filth along; a shallow declivity, across a flat stretch of country for fifty yards, and still unheard and hearing nothing of a suspicious nature, they crept through the blackness of the cloudy night to a deep shell-hole scarcely twenty yards from the woods.

A star shell flared overhead, and they froze to the cold earth like images. The gloomy woods were revealed stark and sinister looking, but there was no sign of the enemy.

"Now, boys," the Lieutenant hissed, "be careful and very, very quiet; we are going into the woods. I'm going first. If anything happens when I get there - Well, Corporal Fraser, you're in command."

They edged themselves to the fringe of trees - was the distance twenty yards or was it five hundred - it seemed miles.

To the south a flare went up, and they flopped motionless - a yard - another. A pair of machine guns chattered to their right and stopped abruptly, and they reached the first tree.

They lay there, listening intently for any sound. None came, save the patter of rain that was beginning to fall, and the occasional rumble of thunder.

"Come on, now," the Lieutenant breathed, "and for Heaven's sake be silent."

They started forward again, pushing cautiously through the woods. The roar of the rain helped to drown out any noise. Then one of the rear men tripped over a dead branch and plunged into a mass of bushes that crackled loudly.

A machine gun broke into fiendish music on their flank, and the party flung itself as one man to the ground. A moment, however, showed that the gun was not aimed towards them, and they went on.

Under cover of the storm they penetrated an unknown distance into the wood. The situation was puzzling - had the Hun abandoned the woods. Lieutenant Smith was perplexed. Were they behind the German lines? He had almost decided to turn back when the affair was suddenly and definitely settled for them.

From ahead of them, as they pushed slowly between rain-soaked trees, came a hoarse, gutteral challenge.

They flung themselves to the ground; then came a sudden, sharp explosion, a spurt of flame and a heavy thud indicated that the grenade had taken effect.

"Down, down, you fools!" the Lieutenant called hoarsely. "Get down and crawl out of here. I'll shoot the man who threw that bomb."

But there is no telling what overwrought and nervy men will do in a crisis. Bang! Another grenade burst closer than the first, showing to the party the position of the enemy.

Lieutenant Smith wasted no time in vain regrets at the action of his men, but dived into a convenient shell-hole. A sudden burst of noise opened up behind them as they crouched down into the crater.

Grenades burst where they had been, and the big Lugar pistols of the Germans barked incessantly.

The movement of many men became audible to the group of nerve-wracked men. The rat-a-tat-tat of machine guns was absent, no doubt the enemy fearing for his comrades.

The patrol lay silent, their only hope being to keep their position secret. Then a heavy body toppled into the shell-hole on top of them. He screamed as a bullet went searing through his heart.

Lieutenant Smith yelled hoarsely to his men to fire, and at the same time he began firing into the darkness whence came the heavy bark of service pistols and the crackle of rifle fire.

He realised that his men were firing and that the grenades were taking their toll of the Hun. Then a vague mass of men loomed above them, and he fired into it.

He laughed hysterically as the killing lead sprayed the group, and he prayed a little as he saw them wilt and dive for shelter. His automatic clicked down on a dead shell, and he realised that they had no more ammunition.

"No more ammunition, Sir," he heard Corporal Fraser snarl; "not a damn thing, Sir, and no bayonet. That you, Williams. What you groaning about? Got you in the arm, eh? Well, use the other one, or you won't see Blighty any more, take it from me. They'll come over any minute. See if that Fritz has got a bayonet on him."

Something smacked on the lip of the crater. Hardly realising what he was doing, Lieutenant Smith reached forward and flung it back.

The grenade went off sharply. A scream ending in a half sob, and then silence.

"Do you surrender, there?" a voice called out from the opposing trench - evidently from an English spoken German officer.

For answer a Lugar pistol spat defiance at the voice. It was Private James with the dead German's revolver. A sharp hiss, the sound of a heavy fall, and Private James grinned at his fluke shot.

"Here, 'Loot,' take this," and he pressed the revolver into the Lieutenant's hand. "I'm going to creep out and get some more 'ammo' and pistols. Those dead Huns will have plenty of them. Oh, for a machine gun," he whispered, as he slipped over the shell-hole. "Give us some covering fire, Loot, they will think we have plenty of 'ammo' left. There's about twenty Huns out here," he hissed, "as dead as a door-nail - here goes."

The Lieutenant covered him with spasmodic firing for what seemed an eternity, then out of the darkness a figure slumped into the shell hole and a hoarse voice gave the information that he had four revolvers, about a hundred rounds of ammunition and about twelve grenades. The men in the hole sighed with relief. "Good boy, James," the Lieutenant said, "I'll remember this when we get back. Now load up, boys, and fire from all directions; they will think we are a large party. Put Williams up against the side - prop him up - now, fire."

The patrol fired to the right and left and to the front. A few desultory shots answered them and a grenade came over, but was thrown too far.

"Good," Lieutenant Smith laughed bitterly, "they have taken to cover; they will attack in the early morning. We'll have to get out of here, lads; there's a few good Huns knocking on the Styx gates right now, and they will want their pound of flesh. How many did you count out there, James," he asked?

"Couldn't see 'em all, sir, but I should say about fifteen of 'em, all dead, sir."

"O.K.," his officer declared grimly, "not a bad bag. How is Williams, Corporal?"

"He's out to it, Sir, bleeding badly, poor chap," he muttered. "Any rum, Sir?"

"Yes. Here give him a drop of this. We will have to get him out of here.

"Lift him over the rear of the hole, and you, Private Erronson and Brody get him back to the lines. We will keep the Hun engaged until you are out of hearing. Be quiet about it, too. Leave your revolvers here, also your grenades; we will give Fritz a lively time before we go. Warn our lads not to fire on us when we return."

As the two men lifted their prostrate comrade over the lip of the crater, the three men kept up an insistent fire, to fool the Hun.

The next question was how to beat a retreat and regain their own lines, as it was obvious that Fritz was holding the line with a minimum of men, and this information would be of incalculable value to H.Q. And yet if they deserted the shell-hole, Fritz's sentries, who were thoroughly alarmed, would sound the alarm that a breakaway was in progress, and a concerted attack by overwhelming numbers would be made to capture the men in possession of such valuable information.

Lieutenant Smith reasoned this out, but decided that he could not leave a man behind, although he knew they would volunteer in an instant and go to their death willingly.

He decided to make a dash for it an hour before dawn. He unfolded his plan to the two men and stressed the urgency of getting through, although the odds were a hundred to one against.

"We're game, Sir," volunteered Private James, taking precedence over his Corporal.

"Game for anything," corrected the Corporal.

"Good." The Lieutenant lapsed into silence and reloaded the Lugar from clips he had stuck in his pocket.

About an hour before dawn the Lieutenant roused his patrol. "They seem quiet now," be whispered. "Come on, lads. You go first. I'll give them a parting volley to let 'em see we are still here."

The Corporal and Private James slipped over the crater lip noiselessly. "Let 'em have it, Sir," hissed the Corporal.

The automatic spat into the darkness ahead, a rifle bullet sank into the ground, and striking a hard substance, whined away in the distance. "Now for it." The officer smiled grimly to himself as he slid over the top of the crater. "They will guess it's a trick in a few minutes, and there'll be hell to play."

As if in answer to his thoughts, a bullet whined overhead, then something stung him in the right side. He gave a shuddering little cough and gasped for breath.

He crawled forward after his two men. Ten yards - twenty yards - then a whispered voice from the darkness. "You all right, Sir."

"Yes, James," he lied. "Got a scratch. Pad me up; I'm bleeding a bit. No. don't cut the uniform - outside will do. Man, don't wave that bandage about as if it was a flag of trace.

They pressed forward, their faces whipped savagely by the branches of the undergrowth, their clothes sodden and muddy. A flare picked them out in a little open space; they had no time to lay down.

Rat-a-tat-tat a machine gun opened out on them. They heard a harsh guttural command, and a big German loomed up not ten paces away on their right. James whipped out his revolver and shot the Hun dispassionately; another appeared in his place. The Corporal's potato masher descended on his face - he went to earth with a mournful little sob. The Lieutenant fired point blank at two more, and then they ran as best they were able for their own lines.

A clattering and hammering broke the stillness of the morning. Back of them was a snarling, growling crescendo of noise - the sharp crack of grenades, the whip and whine of bullets, and the sound of hurrying, stumbling men.

Harsh commands rang out. The Corporal sagged to his knees, coughed and rolled one, with his finger still clutched to the trigger.

"Dead," the Lieutenant screamed to Private James. "They got him clean."

A burly German came rushing at them with lowered bayonet.

Crack, and he stretched out in the mud.

Something like a mad hornet stung the Lieutenant in the fleshy part of the leg. He staggered, his feet dragging painfully; he could hear panting, shouting men at his heels.

Private James stopped to fire into the advancing Huns. They took cover for a moment.

"Go on, Sir, you make for it," yelled James. "Give 'em stacks for me," and Private James stopped and faced the oncoming rush.

The Lieutenant stumbled forward. Ahead were his own countrymen, who hailed news of him. Private James would stop them until he got to his trenches. He was done. Something hit him on the side of the face; he heard a dim explosion and fell savagely to his knees. It was like the "blow from a blacksmith's hammer." He spat out blood and teeth. A numbing pain told him that half his face was gone. There was no pain. A dark mist was settling over him. "Don't fire," he screamed to the men in his trenches, "don't fire."

He rolled over, the bitterness of defeat surging through him.

Then strong hands grasped him and pulled him over the trench. "An officer, quick," he gasped through his torn mouth, as he roused himself from the darkness of the black pit that seemed to yawn beneath him.

Someone was holding his hand, cold water revived his numbed senses and cleared his blood-blinded eyes. "Captain," he muttered, "the line weakly held - German attack down on French sector - I think at Chercey - guess I'm due for leave - cheerio, old bean."

He was starting to wander, but the Captain pulled him back to dim consciousness. "Not yet, old man, not yet," he pleaded.

The Lieutenant licked his shattered lips. "Big attack Chercey - tonight - troops moving from here - watch Chercey."

A moment later grim-faced runners were racing to Headquarters, telephone bells were buzzing and stretcher-bearers were rushing to the aid of the bullet-torn man.

The Captain bent over him again. "A wonderful deed," he

murmured to the officer who was with him. "A Victoria Cross job, at the least."

The Lieutenant's lips moved again. "He's in delirium," and he bent his ear to the tattered lips to listen.

But the Lieutenant was not in delirium exactly. He muttered thickly: "Private James, D.C.M. - Lieutenant Smith wishes to report-: - no men to spare - cheerio! - Cherrio, lads - Marjorie - Marjorie - look after Bibby." And the shattered hero passed into eternal rest.

MY FRENCH BRIDE

I met her as I was coming over the hill. She was sitting there plucking poppies and daisies. She had a huge scarlet and white bunch in her waist. When she saw me coming she pulled her dress over her dainty ankles. I loved her straight away for this, girlish action. As I came abreast of her I stopped and saluted, and, as a means of coming to a better understanding, I suggested that it "tres bien, M'selle."

She answered in French, and said, "Oui Monsieur."

Not being well versed in French, and taking this for an excuse, I sat down on the grass beside her. She continued picking flowers, so I helped her. When handing them to her our hands met. I could not restrain myself. I looked into her eyes and saw a smile. In a mad fit of passion I threw my arms around her and kissed her eyes, her lips; her brow. She hung in my arms like some poor drooping flower.

My little sweetheart; I assured her; it will be alright. Do not worry. We shall get married and you will come back with me to sunny Australia. I crushed her closer still. I could feel her heart beating madly; my own was driving all the hot blood to my head.

"Why don't you speak?" I pleaded, looking into her eyes. Her eyes avoided mine; she turned her head. After a few moments she spoke, this time, to my surprise, in English. "But Father -" she began. "Take me to him at once," I commanded, "Come on, little one."

I gave her my hand and helped her to get up. After fifteen minutes' walking, we came to her father's home. She ushered me into his library, and asked me to sit down while she went to look for him. I sat down till she left the room, and then I practised "right hooks" and "straight lefts" with my image in the big bevelled mirror.

Ah! Ah! I thought; if he does not grant me my request I will kill him. At last he came, and walked straight up to me. I got on my defence. He threw his arms around me. I prepared to strike; he hugged me closer still. I lifted my head to look him squarely in the eyes, then - then he kissed me, right cheek first, then left cheek.

I remembered the French style of greeting, and dropped my hands. With a voice choking with emotion I said, "Monsieur - your daughter--"

"Yes, yes," he interrupted; "I know - she has gone to prepare."

He took my arm and led me to the sideboard, and with cool, sparkling wine he toasted my future. He gave me a fine cigar and began to tell me what he proposed to do.

"In a few hours," he said, "you shall be married; you have my blessing. Further, I ask you to accept this place as your home. Everything is yours; in the strong room you will find all the money you need for the next fifty years."

I fell on my knees and thanked him for his kindness. He raised me to my feet and said: "Monsieur, it will be a great alliance - France and Australia - Come, let us drink."

At last she came arrayed in her bridal attire. I kissed her sweet lips, once, twice; thrice. I heard as in a dream my future father-in-law saying, "Come, the car is waiting."

He led the way outside. In the bright afternoon sunlight a magnificent car was waiting; two gorgeous servants helped us to our seats. It did not take us long to reach the church. I signed my name and went to the altar. The joy that was mine brought a mist before my eyes, a band of iron encircled my throat.

"Will you take this woman?" the minister asked. "Yes, yes," I answered.

I produced the ring and slipped it on her delicate finger. The wedding march boomed out as we walked up the aisle. As we were getting into the car my father-in-law stepped up to me and handed me a bag of gold.

I said, "Sir, how can I thank you - "

"Hush! hush! take it - the Alliance -"

I put out my hand . . . and heard the doctor say, "His pulse is rapid tonight, Nurse; what have you been giving him to eat?"

I opened my eyes and looked around. It seemed to be the same hospital, my bed-clothes were on the floor, my pillow was tied in a knot. A few beds further up I could hear two men arguing. One was saying: "I'll bet you ten bob that the Alliance was broken between Germany and Italy." He rattled the money in his hand. I hear the chink of the money to this very day. My agony was completed when I heard the doctor say, "That band will have to practise further away from the hospital in future."

THE LIMEHOUSE PARADE

So to the city of enchantment to forget the past, in the whirlpool of life and laughter - Paris, the city of dead hopes, and sin unashamed - Paris, the home of culture and learning and the heart of Bohemia. I would take what it had to offer and regret at my leisure. So ran my thoughts as the train steamed into the famous centre. I took myself off to a modest little flat in the Rue Carmel, a quaint, sequestered little street close to the banks of the Seine, where the noise and clatter of the city rarely penetrated. A sour-visaged old crone showed me up the narrow stairs to my room, and requested the rent and made arrangements for my breakfast.

Early next morning I was up and about, wandering fancy free wherever fate or curiosity tempted me to go. I rather incline to the machination of fate guiding my feet down to the Limehouse Parade, for it is indeed wonderful how one single hour of idleness can lend itself to opportunity and convert itself into a period of great learning. Fate and the devil walk hand in hand along the Limehouse, so the forsaken women of Bohemia will tell you, and it is mostly fate that treats you shabbily and leaves you. The devil of the Limehouse is a cruel master, tracking his victims, and occasionally leading them to the banks of the Seine, to forget their troubles in the bosom of the turbid waters. It is not until you study the inner life of the Limehouse that you realise what a complex problem the social life of a big city is. You will see well-dressed business men and flashly-dressed criminals jostle each other for pavement space, and an immaculately-dressed dude greeting his latest flame across the way with an old-world flourish of the hat, the while his fingers search the pocket of an unsuspecting stranger. Men from the four corner of the earth ply their business, doubtful and otherwise, and cunning, shifty-eyed

eyed Apaches take the air, and anything else that is easy to get without much labor. You listen with compassion to the broken-down jeweller, who attributes his poverty to the fact that he tried to sell engagement rings at £13 and got no buyers. You give him a franc to help feed his wife and innumerable children, receive his blessing, and feel very benevolent, and then discover that half the inhabitants of the Limehouse have a new and original tale to tell you of dying wives and bad luck. Behind half-closed doors sit the painted women of easy virtue, the flotsam of Bohemia, and high in the attic above them, the Chinese magnate and his lesser compatriot, the peanut vendor, shake dice and smoke opium and dream fantastic dreams of the East. Ragged urchins, world wise and under-fed, fossick in the gutters, much the same as urchins the world over, in the hopes of salvaging something edible. A drunken woman shrieks her imprecations of a wine seller who has denied her, and a mangy dog sends up a mournful wail to the house-tops. This is the view of the Limehouse, and is how it impresses a stranger. A gendarme, on his beat, appears, and here and there little groups of men disperse and sidle down dark alley-ways, painted faces peep out and withdraw quickly and doors slam, for the mortal enemy of the Limehouse is about. The drunken woman steadies in her gait, and tries to look engaged with her handkerchief. Deeper down other elements are at work. The crimes of Paris are born and fostered here, by grim, cunning men who stake life and liberty for the luxury of an easy existence.

A rattle of brass instruments, sadly out of tune, and the shrill voice of a girl singing a quaint old song attracted my attention. I sauntered slowly along the Parade until I came to a low-class musical-hall. Tendering my admission fee, I entered and sat down. A small stage, garishly decorated in gold and green, was the only splash of color in the sombre, forbidding interior, the seats were hard and backless, the roof grimed with smoke and filth. The piece de resistance was a one-act drama, by the whole company, of high life in a world far removed from the Limehouse. It was the old story of the eternal triangle, two men and a woman, a suicide, tears, and mutual forgiveness. I acclaimed the acting of the heroine with enthusiasm; she favored me with an exaggerated bow and a toss of the head, then the curtain descended on all the glory of green and gold, and the audience dispersed slowly, sadly it seemed, as if loath to return to their haunts of darkness.

M'SIEUR GIBRAUD

Some few days after my visit to the Limehouse I was sitting at one of the little tables outside the Cafe Vivre, in the Rue Carmonde. It is a delightful spot to spend a few idle hours. It is situated right in the fashionable quarters of Paris, and is the early-morning promenade of the elite. Tall trees and green lawns flank the pavement, and lend an air of detachment to this delightful place. For a few francs you can mimic your prosperous brother, and sip rare wine and be at case with the world. One would never guess, to look at the gaily-dressed crowd, that a few years ago there had been war, and that the people now idling the time away had helped it to a successful issue. It is only we who saw the French at war that can realise the undying patriotism of the French people. Delicately nurtured women nursed in the hospitals and imposed on themselves the most menial tasks. All sorts and conditions of people allied themselves with but one object in view; mere girls became responsible for public duties, carrying a penalty that many years of peace will not throw off. Yet one would never guess, were it not for the number of men who pass wearing the scars and medals of war, and the young girls with the old eyes and strange, careworn features, that spoke of weary, anxious days, that war had ever visited this glorious land, or that it had ever imposed its penalties. I was about to vacate my scat when my attention was drawn to a gentleman, who detached himself from the moving mass of people and felt his way, cautiously, between the tables. I noticed his face was fearfully scarred and that he was blind. A waiter came hurrying along and asked me would I shift to another seat on the opposite side of the table, as M'sieur Gibraud was a regular customer, and, owing to his affliction, always liked to occupy the same seat. I agreed readily, and asked M'sieur would he join me in a glass. Over a convivial glass no introduction was necessary, and so before very long we were on very friendly terms. His manner and bearing appealed to me. His speech was cultured and refined, and his personality very engaging. From everyday topics the conversation turned to war, and it was then I heard M'sieur Gibraud's story. Let me tell it to you as he told it to me.

"Yes. M'sieur, war is a ghastly business. Many times have I tried to discover the reason why men march out to battle, with naked swords, to fight their fellow-man, who are the same as they, although perhaps with different languages and different customs, but with the same hopes and fears and the same desires. It is the beast in man that makes him kill and hate the other man, who is divided only from him by a geographical line. I say the beast, M'sieur, because in war we mimic the ape, whom we are supposed to have evolved from; in fact we put the ape to shame, for we bring science to our aid and commit ghastly deeds, in the name of humanity. In this recent war my firm conviction was that the Allies, and they alone, had a just cause, and that our enemies were the brutes. I recently met an old friend of mine, a German of good education, and I told him this, and he persisted that his country was right and that we were wrong, and a very convincing argument he favored me with. But I would not be convinced, M'sieur. Patriotism blinded the argument, and so I am no further advanced, and he left me in anger. I was taught from early childhood that France was the only country in the world worth thinking of; that French history was more glorious than all other nations combined. I have been spoon-fed with it: to think otherwise would be ridiculous; to give voice to my opinions, I if I doubted it, would be to condemn myself, and so, M'sieur. we have war. I myself have suffered grievously. Life to me is a set routine, as I cannot escape the darkness. My features are scarred and hideous to behold; even in the street I feel people shudder as they pass me. I inspire sympathy. But what is sympathy, M'sieur - merely the child of pity, as unpractical as it is genuine. I am a cast-off of Mars. I went out in the early pride of my manhood, not on a killing expedition, but on an errand of mercy, and I return thus, sightless and helpless - a somebody for someone to pity and be sorry for. You will follow my reasoning when I tell you how this happened. I was a doctor, and at the outbreak of war was called to the colors and detailed to go to the front with my regiment - of course, in a professional capacity.

I was at Verdun in that terrific attack at the latter end of 1916. Our men were being slaughtered by thousands, and we were short-handed and could only attend to those who had a hope of being saved; the badly-wounded were left to die. Ah, M'sieur, they were dreadful days, and it wracked my nerves to see brave men dying in agony, when, if we had more time, they could possibly have been saved. I had for my operating theatre a little steel-lined house, situated in the corner of the fort. It had been used for an explosives storeroom in the days of peace, and the only opening for ventilation was a little porthole, set high up near the ceiling. The afternoon I speak of was in November, and, as you know, the section at that time was reasonably quiet. A young lad had been brought in by the stretcher-bearers, and I recognised him as a college chum. He had been injured internally, and was unconscious. My professional pride and training told me he could be saved by an immediate operation, and I resolved to do this at once, as several unprofessional little matters had come into the fight with death. I had loved the same girl as he, and as she had favored him with her attentions, you will realise M'sieur, that although I was not doing my duty I was at least human, for it was my place only to bandage the wounds and assuage the pain to a certain extent. I called my orderly and told him to lock and bolt the door and to remain outside and guard against an entry of my superiors, unless, of course, they demanded an entry, for by performing this operation I was transgressing the rules and orders of my commandant, and knew that if I was discovered it would mean the loss of my reputation, and that to a doctor is everything. My task was progressing favorably. I had located the piece of metal that was killing the boy, and before long I had removed it. Then, M'sieur, a dreadful thing happened; a shell flung far from the rear of the enemy's trench crashed through the roof. I saw it, M'sieur; I saw the poor, mutilated form of the boy smashed beyond recognition, even before I realised my own danger, for in a second such as this one sees many things. Then came the crash. I felt myself lifted bodily upwards and outwards; I felt stinging pains in my face, and then I lost consciousness. It was many weeks later before I realised what had happened and then I did not realise I was blind, for impressed on my mind was the scene in the storeroom, and I could see it as vivid in detail as the moment it happened. You see my face, M'sieur; that is the reward of mercy. My sightless eyes are the blessing of heaven, for to me it has blotted out war, and there is mercy in darkness.

"That is war for you, M'sieur. There is no glory, no mercy in war, and I content myself when I am inclined to be rebellious against my fate by coming to it here, and let people see the wreck of the man that was,. and help to impress on them that war is hideous and cruel. Look around you and sec if the people are older by years - even the young are wise beyond their years. Now, M'sieur, I come to the end of my story. Three days ago I sat at this very table, and here on my right, at that next table, several people were in earnest conversation. I recognised the voice of one; it was my patient's sweetheart, and I heard her say she was proud of her man; he was brave to die on the field of battle for France. I had my back to them, M'sieur, and I turned my sightless eyes and scarred face for them to see, and I heard her say, 'Oh, look, the poor fellow! How horrible! Fancy being like that!' And I heard her give a half-frightened, surprised little laugh. Poor girl, she knows no different, and had not know it was me. How could she know that I had sacrificed my sight, my career, my all, for her man, for he, poor fellow, was posted as missing, and under the circumstances how could I disclose my identity, and tell her of his last hours?"

He drummed the marble-topped table with his fingers, and I thought I saw him smile.

"Your story, M'sieur, is very sad, as you say; there is no mercy in war itself, but your act shows that individually there is mercy and understanding."

"Yes," he interrupted, "you are right in what you say, but that is not all. I will leave yon now, M'sieur. If you ask Francois, the waiter, he will tell you the rest of my story."

I escorted him on to the pavement and bade him adieu, and my heart went out to the poor, faltering wreck, Monsieur Gibraud. I returned to the table and called Francois over to me. "'You know M'sieur Gibraud?" I questioned, slipping a coin into his hands "Tell me what is worrying him."

"Did M'sieur tell you to ask me about it?" Francois asked.

"Yes; he did not complete the story."

"Ah," whispered Francois, "he never does. Yon know he was court-martialled for disobeying orders, and severely censured. And did he tell you of Madam Schultzer? He met her here three days ago; she sat at that table to your right. He knew her voice, and asked me to describe her to him. I have reason to think, if M'sieur will permit of me saying, that he once loved her. She is now married to a German, and you, M'sieur, will understand his feelings."

"Is that all, Francois," I said.

"No, M'sieur, Madam called me over just before she left, and asked me to give the poor poliu another drink at her husband's expense. It is my business to be obliging, M'sieur, and so I accepted it with a smile; but I could not insult my old captain so, and never mentioned it to him; but he heard it, for he said, after they had gone, 'Merci, Francois, I understand.' You see, M'sieur, I know Captain Gibraud's story. I was his orderly at Verdun, and gave my evidence against him at the trial. Of course, I was compelled to."

"Thank you, Francois," I said; "you will give my respects to the Captain tomorrow, and tell him that I understand why there is no mercy in war."

A SHATTERED ROMANCE

A poor, lonely, faltering figure, hobbling pitifully along, step by cautious step, as if afraid to trust his pain racked body to suffer the jar of contact with the pavement; a painful pause, as if undecided to go further, a grim, grave smile playing around his torture twisted mouth, his eyes sunk well back into their sockets, but bright with faith and courage. His clothes had seen better days, worn in parts, and shining with excessive wear, they were still neat and clean. His battered old hat was jammed carelessly on his head, and gave him an air of recklessness that was not in keeping with his faltering feet. He paused at the corner to borrow a match, and lighting his cigarette, he passed from my vision. But "tap, tap," I could hear his stick make contact with the pavement, long after he had passed. Just a lonely Digger wending his way through life, with no hope of recovery, and little to make life bright, and so he would plod along until that great reveille in heaven, when the halt will become well and the weak strong. But let me tell you his romance, and for the sake of the story let us call him "Bluey," for that was his nom de guerre in those days, when any one worth while laid claim to nick names. invented to meet the demands of comradeship, and for the sake of distinction. Bluey was runner attached to a battalion that was engaged in heavy fighting at the latter end of 1916. His duties carried him into various places, away from the lines. And apart from being a good soldier it was also desirable to be a good diplomat - for the French people were at times easily offended, ow ing to our free and easy style of making our wants and desires known. But Bluey had never incurred the displeasure of a Frenchman or Frenchwoman, and having a fair smattering of French to aid him, he was generally the chosen man for many little missions at the back of the lines. This brought him in touch with a family who lived in the little village of Estairs behind our lines, and rumour had it that Bluey was courting one of the daughters. Often he was missing from his billet, and would return late at night unobserved by his officer, and he generally managed to wangle village leave on some flimsy pretext. We did not grudge Bluey his little pleasure, for he was an altogether likeable chap, and very obliging, and as there were others of us who had sweethearts in the village, he was a very handy medium for the exchange of greetings when leave from our billets was not granted. Then came the attack at Fleurbaix, with its nights of death and horror. Many of the lads who had sweet-hearts passed along the long road into eternal night - but Bluey survived, and at first opportunity visited his rendezvous. We noted a change in Bluey from that night, he returned to the billet with a hang-dog expression on his face, and the look of a man who had suffered a rude awakening. We chided him on the loss of his erstwhile good spirits, and enquired the cause, but he was noncommittal in his answers, as if he wished to avoid a discussion, and there was a cause. Marmette, his sweetheart, had not shown any pleasure at his return, not that she did not care for the lad, for he was good enough for any full-blooded lass to rave over, but he had come upon her in rather strange circumstances. Thinking, to surprise her, he had stolen around to the little side window of her boudoir. Peeping in under the curtains he espied Marmette kneeling on the floor, with a telephone receiver to her ear, and speaking into the mouthpiece in a strange guttural language, that Bluey knew was not the French tongue. Her face was transformed, and she spoke earnestly and quickly, as if afraid of detection. That she was a spy did not enter his calculations, and feeling guilty at the intrusion, he rapped gently on the window pane. Marmette sprang to her feet, and pulling a tiny revolver from her blouse, covered the window, and demanded to know who was there. Backing away into the darkness, he went to the side door and knocked. A very pale and frightened looking Marmette opened the door and admitted him. "Buffoon," she chided in French, "was you at my window! You scared me. I was - I was dressing." Bluey disclaimed all knowledge of the occurrence, but he noticed that Marmette and her father were eyeing him very closely, as if ready to close with him. He also noticed that Marmette - his pretty

Marmette, as he fondly called her - held something in her hands that she was careful to keep hidden in the folds of her dress. His suspicions now thoroughly aroused, and feeling that he was in a corner that would demand all his diplomatic resources, he set to work to allay, the best way he could, their well-founded suspicions of what he had seen. He noticed that her father was not as old as perhaps he should be, for he rarely moved from the fireplace, and never entered into any conversation between his daughter and Bluey. Tonight this fact struck him as mighty strange, more so when he noticed a tiny fringe of black hair bordering the thatch of worthy grey hairs, that her father laid claim to. After a strained attempt at conversation that lasted well over an hour, Bluey bid them good night, and wended his way billet-wards.

After a sleepless night and a morning of torture, he at last made bold enough to convey to his superior his well-founded suspicions, and told the events of the previous night. The officer expressed surprise and pleasure after listening to Bluey's recital, and complimented him on his clever discovery, which, under any other circumstances would have been very complimentary, but at the present juncture was nothing less than gall and wormwood. A platoon was at once ordered to stand by to proceed to the village and make investigations, and Bluey was detailed to act as guide to his officer. Reaching their destination, the platoon formed a cordon round the house, and the officer, with a poor display of taste, detailed Bluey to go and make the purport of their visit known, but fortunately he escaped that indignity, for hardly had the officer spoken, when the ping of a bullet was heard, and the captain clapped his hand to his right arm. Taking what cover offered, the order was given to open fire, and a hail of bullets was soon spattering around the house of Bluey's beloved. The firing from the house still continued, and a moan here and there gave token of the marksmanship of Marmette and her decrepit father. The firing from the house gradually ceased, and the Captain passed the order around to fix bayonets, and close in on the house. After a fierce struggle Marmette and her father - now stripped of his disguise - were captured. To Bluey bad fallen the lot of capturing his erstwhile sweetheart, and in the struggle that ensued he had to handle her roughly, for she fought like a wild cat - and cursed him and his countrymen. A full plant for sending and receiving messages from behind the lines was discovered in Marmette's room, and their guilt was proved. At the court-martial Bluey gave the necessary evidence to condemn Marmette and her father to death by shooting, and was severely reprimanded for his association with her. He formed one of the squad selected for the firing party, and the pressure of his finger on the trigger helped to send Marmette or her father to their doom, for they sat back to back, and blindfolded. There is little to tell now. Bluey went up to battle the next day, and fought as only a man in his unenviable position could fight. He was the first over the top, and hacked and tore his way to glory, counting not the cost, but courting the death that he welcomed. A shell hurled him into the lap of death, but the fickle jade scorned him who welcomed her, and passed him out a wreck for life, and the tap, tap, of his stick will sound in the busy street; people will hurry past him; later on children will fear him. The young girls will pity him, charity will be doled sparingly to him, and his eternal nightmare will be: A blind-folded figure on a chair at twenty paces, a pressure of the trigger. Marmette, his love, whose only sin was her love of country, a lifeless heap of clay.

NANETTE

"You know," said Mark Connell, puckering his brows and imbibing deeply from a glass that he held m his hand with the careless grace of a connoisseur, "there is nothing quite so good as sparkling hock or music as starter of romance. In fact, to my mind, they are indispensable. I speak from experience, for it was through the influence of these two things that my short-lived romance with Nanette began. I met her, as you know, in Bruges, while on special duty there. I dropped into a little cafe on the Rue Plaza, late one afternoon, for a meal and a taste of this stuff." He gazed thoughtfully into the glass. "The waiter, a real treasure of a chap, sensed that I would not say No to pleasant company, and led me to a table where Nanette was seated, nibbling biscuits, and looking real melancholy. At first she appeared to be indignant at my intrusion, or perhaps she was annoyed with the waiter for assuming that she would not object. But these things come easy on the Continent, where strict introductions are unnecessary, and before long I was pouring her out a glass of hock. Francois -the waiter- having tactfully retired to the seclusion of the grill room, I soon had her talking about things that interested her, as the hock seemed to loosen her tongue. She was a most diverting little Miss, very vivacious, with a wide range of subjects at her command to lend interest to her conversation. We completed our impromptu little At Home, and being naturally nervous, and feeling as yet on insecure ground, I did not like to suggest a run in the car, or a theatre. As you understand, I felt that I was only being tolerated, for the time being, and reasoned that a dashing girl of her type would have a host of followers. I tried to pluck up courage to ask her, but after several attempts I gave it up.

Francois -the waiter- put in an appearance then, and greasing his palm with a ten franc note, I appealed to him, by gesture, to arrange things for me. As I said before, he was a perfect waiter, and aided by my inspiring tip, he grasped the situation at once, and delicately conveyed to Nanette that Monsieur was a stranger in Bruges, and was not quite conversant with the entertainments that offered for otherwise disengaged young couples. Well, after Francois putting the words in my mouth like that, and starting the offensive, as it were, I necessarily had to maintain the attack, and took up the discourse by offering to accompany Mademoiselle somewhere, perhaps where we could find a little diversion. Could I suggest the Follies Dance? I had been there previously, and it was the only place I knew. To my surprise Nanette was delighted with the suggestion, and signified her readiness to accompany me by offering me her arm. She favored the waiter with a brief, pleased little smile, and I, gratified beyond expression, gave him another twenty francs, as a reward for his most excellent services.

We spent the afternoon at the Follies, dancing. The floor, the music, the surroundings and my partner, were all completely in accord with my taste. I'm afraid it all went to my head, not being used to it for some considerable time. The music and the appealing softness of my partner made me reckless, and in the interval between dances, I must say I flirted outrageously for so short an acquaintance.

Nothing lost, Nanette encouraged me up to a certain point, and then let me cool down. You know, I felt like a man dangling on the end of a rope, but it was an exhilarating experience while it lasted. But I will always regret making an ass of myself, for after one particularly exquisite waltz I proposed to her. Yes, I know it is laughable, it is to me now, after all these years, but I assure you it was very sincere while it lasted and perhaps if the Continental code of morals and their sense of humor was identical with ours, I would not be the care-free bachelor you see me tonight, and instead of a quiet bachelor evening such as we are having, I would have a gay little vixen of a wife to be the hostess, and measure out this elixir of life." He gazed into the glass reflectively.

"However, that is the romance. The various incidentals that led up to the shattering of it are amusing. Mind, I am speaking now when time has softened the memory of the various shocks I experienced. I can sip good wine and listen to better music, quite unperturbed, since that time, for I realise that, after all, a wine and music romance and a pretty girl romance is very transitory, and can last just so long as good sense and matured reason are not the strong points of one's characteristics.

"After the dance, and at my suggestion, we returned to the little cafe for dinner. Francois ushered us to our table, and made himself most obliging on our behalf. He was very diplomatic, and a wonderful tactician, always ready to step into the breach if the conversation flagged, and always ready with some little service that softened our embarrassed moments, for which I was naturally very grateful. Although, I must confess, it was the first time in my eventful life that I had any love affairs managed, and it was incongrous but under the circumstances, acceptable. A delightful dinner disposed of, our thoughts turned to the evening's entertainment, and not lacking now, I purchased an evening paper, and told Nanette to choose her place of amusement. After much discussion on the merits of the various plays, she eventually decided on going to see a light comedy at the Caliph. I must confess it was a happy choice for me, although it must have been very discomforting for Nanette. It was the usual froth and bubble affair, but with a rather clever plot and numerous delectable little sketches.

It was during the progress of one of these sketches in the second act that I began to feel as if I was personally interested in the affairs of a particularly passionate young fellow who met his swain in similar circumstances to my meeting Nanette. The dance and all followed, only, of course, curtailed to a considerable extent in comparison to ours. The ardor of their little dance prepared me for what was to follow. As in all true musical comedy he proposed, only I must say in fairness to myself, it was of a much more farcical nature than my fervent outpouring. I stole a glance at Nanette, and the rising color in her cheeks showed plainly her feelings and embarrassment. You can imagine mine. I felt as if I ought to do something sensible, and a desire possessed me to call out to stop this prostitution of a romance that I was then wrapped up in I squeezed Nanette's arm to give her a sense of comradeship and encouragement, and suggested that we leave the theatre. She readily acquiesced, and once out in the fresh air I felt better, and apologised for taking her to such a show - although it was no fault of mine.

"The next few days I spent dreaming and planning, and looked to the future when our little affair would mature into an engagement. You see, by this time I was thoroughly infatuated with her.

"A call back to my battalion hastened matters for me, and, before I left, I had the pleasure of placing a valuable ring on her finger, in token of my regard for her. I was to return to Bruges in eight days' time, and so the parting was not so poignant as it could have been, had I been going away for a long period. On my return I wended my way around to my favorite rendezvous, as it was yet early afternoon. Francois was not at his customary post to greet me, and so I strolled inside, and went to my usual table. Hardly had I taken my seat when I fancied I heard Nanette laugh, and Francois' voice remonstrating with her. I listened, and heard Nanette say in a querulous voice, 'Silly, he will not return. He is but a buffoon.' And then Francois came to serve me. On seeing who it was he stopped in his stride like a wounded animal, faltered, and came on again. His eyes bulged, and by his guilty expression I instantly saw that I was the buffoon under discussion. It was an unenviable moment, but I rose from the table and demanded Francois to bring Nanette to me, and give an explanation. It was a very contrite pair that stood before me, for judgment. I was about to soundly thrash Francois for his impudence, and advanced on him to put into execution my desire, but Nanette put herself between he and I, and asked me to cease, as Francois was her husband. She confessed it was all a miserable hoax, and of her doing. I did not, could not, under the circumstances, ask any apology or explanation, as it is one thing to talk to a waiter, and another thing to talk to the husband of the woman you love." Connell lit a cigarette, pursed his lips, and blew the smoke ceilingwards. Crossing his long legs he regarded me from between half closed eyes, and continued:

"That evening is one I shall never forget. With my house falling around my feet like a pack of cards you can imagine how I felt about the whole affair. Feeling in no mood for reflection, and with a desire to get my revenge, even if only against myself, for being such an ass, I went and booked a seat at the Caliph, and saw the show out to the bitter end. The sketch in the second act was exactly my romance, only, of course, with more indelicate suggestion. My one regret to this day, if one can regret an educative experience, is that I was fool enough to leave the theatre that night with Nanette. The whole miserable hoax would have been transparent to me, had I stayed, as Nanette's embarrassment plainly showed that she was nervous of the revelation that was being unfolded before our eyes. I learned afterwards that it was a popular form of entertainment with a certain class of people, to catch the stray coin of unsuspecting idiots like myself, who, in moments of relaxation left themselves wide open to the potent influence of the bachelor-snaring triangle - wine, music, and pretty girls.

"That is my romance, Snellgrave, old chap, and always remember that many a cynic has been made by the futile virtues of lost opportunity. That is why I am still a bachelor."

A TRAGEDY OF LOVE AND WAR

Towards the end of the year 1917, a dark and memorable year for us, the good Sureat Harmonger lived on his neat little estate in Flanders.

He and his family, the good Madame Harmonger and his pretty daughter Mademoiselle Nina Harmonger, and a couple of old retainers, were happy and contented enough, although their beloved country was at death grips with an insistent and an almost hereditary foe - Germany.

It was true indeed that the hated enemy had passed through these fair lands, and had bivouacked in the fields, and even taken possession of the Chateau Harmonger for a brief period, but at a given signal and as though by magic they had disappeared almost overnight, without bloodshed, without slaughter, and without ravaging and destroying the fair fields, that at the time of this story lay asleep under the deep pall of winter. It was said that the advancing enemy had thrust too far forward, and so disorganised his rear communications, and of a necessity he had had to retreat, or withdraw to a more favourable spot to give battle.

Some of the peasants regretted their premature departure, for they had money to spend, did those Germans, and under the firm hand of Prussian discipline they did not molest the populace, and it is to be said regretfully that patriotism is a very shallow thing among many when a few paltry francs are concerned.

While Papa Harmonger was not one of these half-hearted patriots, he had, let it be said under compulsion, housed a number of officers, who had paid him well, even though it was in German marks, for there were in those early days ways and means of converting enemy money, and Papa Harmonger was well content and satisfied with the manner in which he and his household had been treated by his country's enemy. Of an evening he would sit at the window of the chateau and gaze into the western sky, where lurid flashes of light, and the low rumble as of distant thunder, spoke of war, of slaughter, of death, of maimed bodies and the soul of civilisation in awful travail.

In these pensive moments his mind would often wander to the enemy officers who had shared his hospitable roof, for, after the war, they had promised to come back.

"When we are once more friends, M'sieur," one handsome young officer had assured him, and he had noticed the quick look of approval that he gave pretty Nina, and the lingering handshake, that Nina did not resist.

But that must never be, he had said to himself on numerous occasions; it could not be. He was a German, although doubtless a worthy lad in nil other respects, but to marry his Nina -his only child- never!

Had Nina been a boy, as he had wished, he would be fighting alongside his countrymen, and had he been young enough himself, he would be there also. Well, well, God was good in giving him a daughter instead of a son, and in that, good Mama Harmonger agreed, for she at last felt that she had been vindicated for presenting a daughter instead of the expected and longed-for son, and was not backward to force the point home in a jolly, homely way on any and every opportune occasion that presented itself. Nina herself had not been the same bright demoiselle since the Germans had departed. At times she was moody, and despondent, for she was at an impressionable age, and, being college educated, had advanced ideas that tended to the romantic, Notwithstanding, life at the chateau was worth living; full of contentment, with only the distant war to blemish the life of the little community, Three years came and went, the cycle of Summer, Winter and Spring - then the drab, drear winter of 1917, when the countryside fell under the spell of rain, snow and mud,

The furious, ominous coughing of the shells came closer, the papers from Paris were not sounding an optimistic note, and day and night long lines of ambulance waggons rumbled over the rough, uneven roadway, through the village, back to the sea coast. Thousands of men choked the narrow thoroughfares, some going up to battle with a jaunty air, others staggering blindly onwards, and always the sinister waggons coming back, until one day it seemed they could go no further, and the powers in command established a dressing station in the Town Hall. This was situated in the main thoroughfare of the village, and about a kilometre from the Chateau Harmonger.

Nina, with the true instinct of her sex, offered her services to the Commandant of the clearing station, and to the intense gratification of her proud father and consenting mama, she was accepted as a voluntary aid, to attend the wounded and supply them with little comforts and attentions. They were days of pride to all in the chateau, for no one was of age to participate in the war, and Nina by her humble service represented the household's sole contribution to the war in the way of man power.

Returning from her duties at all hours of the night, after a full day, did not dull the bright beauty of Nina, rather it had the opposite effect, for she now had a definite purpose in life.

She tended the wounded of both friend and enemy, and it was to be noted that from every wounded German she came in contact with, her first question was to enquire as to the whereabouts of the Saxon regiments. She spoke German fluently, and so inspired confidence in her questioning.

It was during the second week of the battle that Nina returned home one night with a new light in her eyes that was not unnoticed by her father, and on his enquiring as to if she was well, her breathless answer gave the truth to his shocked senses as no other thing could. "Father," she said, "Karl's regiment is in the line up on this front. If – if - he is wounded and captured I may see him again."

The words fell from her lips naturally, but they. stabbed to her father's heart with a sharp thrust that left him weak and faint. So that was the reason of her service. True, it was not disloyalty to love an enemy soldier, but why, why had it not been one of her own countrymen?

That night Papa Harmonger knelt before the little shrine and prayed to Our Lady that it might not be, prayed into the early dawn that the God of War would see fit not to bring this calamity on his house- prayed that the handsome young officer be not killed, but maimed or disfigured so that his little Nina would not recognise him and so save the prestige and honour of his family and his home. Selfish, vindictive, who will condemn, for underlying the conflicting emotions in Papa Harmonger's breast, was the undying patriotism of his race, the love of country, the unsullied honour of his ancestors who had died and suffered for their country, his inherited hatred of the enemy as a class, and his peculiar loyalty to a generous, honourable enemy - an enemy who was doing his duty for his Fatherland gallantly and well, and who had shared the hospitality of his roof; nay, and had enslaved the heart of his precious child, Nina.

In the early light of dawn he went to bed and, to the mocking crescendo of rumbling shells up at the front, cursed the war and his heritage; but said to himself: "It must not be, it must not be. It will not be."

Then came the dread day - there was increased activity in the inferno up further. Great sounds rend the heavens. Artillery waggons dashed across the fields, planes droned overhead, new troops moved up over the open fields, for the word had gone forth, it was whispering in the wind in the crash of shells, in the eyes of the fresh troops pushing forward, in the hurried rattle of shell waggons, "the British and French were advancing."

Troops were billeted everywhere, men with the light of battle in their eyes, and the determination to win in thir souls; and still the wnggons returned down the Iong road with their sorry burden of human wreckage.

Nina was seldom at home these days - she had her scanty meals at the dressing station, and snatched a few hours' rest, when the human wastage was not so plentiful. Then came the blow. It was late afternoon, a dim sun was sinking below the horizon, when Papa Hannonger saw her coming up the drive, half running, and stumbling as though in a frenzy of excitement, and he knew. He knew that down in the village her lad lay on a stretcher and that she had seen him. He knew that her first words would be of Karl. "Good God," he groaned inwardly, and turned from the window, As in a trance he saw his face in the mirror. It was deadly white and grim. He crossed to a bureau and from a drawer brought forth an old pistol, and handled it in an abstracted, almost disinterested, manner.

He stared guiltily into the mirror and then a summons at the door brought him to the reality of their tragedy. He placed the pistol in his pocket and made his way downstairs.

Nina greeted him and gasped out her simple story. "Papa," she whispered, "he is here in the village - Karl. I am so happy; he is hardly wounded at all - a wound in the leg, a mere nothing," she said happily.

"Father, what is wrong? You are ill?" she exclaimed as she saw her father sway drunkenly.

"No, Nina, I must sit down," he assured her. "I am tired!"

She sat alongside her father on the couch,

"Father," she said excitedly, "I am in charge of his ward tonight, when the sister goes off duty - and then" - it struck the old man like a bolt from the blue - "I am going to bring him here."

"But, Nina-"

"It's all right, Papa," she interrupted. "I have got an old uniform and no one will know. I will hide him in the cellar. No one will suspect us, and it will be all right," she concluded simply, as she met her father's eyes.

They sat there in silence for a long time - the old man a true patriot, the young, confiding girl, also a true patriot, a patriot to her country, with loyalty to her man, with the call of young love in her being, that knew no sacrifice too great or too small for that love.

"You will bring him here?" The father spoke slowly. "Tonight?" he asked in a low voice. "Nina, you are aiding the enemy; it is not right."

"But, father, he will not fight again, Poor Karl is sick of it all. He is wounded, and, father, she said simply, "I promised to marry him."

The old man hung his head. So that was it. His daughter, his pride, his patriotism, where was it all now? What did it count, in the face of two young people who were in love?

He had no personal hatred of the young German officer until he heard those words, but what could he do? Report his daughter to the authorities? Demand the young German's removal from the hospital to another base, and by so doing cast suspicion on Nina? He could do nothing. In a low voice he agreed falteringly to his daughter's proposal to bring the German to his roof.

Nina arranged the transfer of the wounded officer with little difficulty, and, apart from a frenzied hue and cry soon after his disappearance, the incident quickly died down and was forgotten as another one of those little unsolved mysteries of the war zone.

Papa Harmonger greeted his unwelcome guest in a distant, old-world manner, and Mama Harmonger, after recovering from her surprise, accorded him the courtesy that the occasion demanded, being, as he was, a guest of her Nina.

The cellar was made snug and comfortable, and at night time when the blinds were drawn and the servants retired to bed, he came to the upper parts of the house.

On occasions such as these Papa Harmonger would retire to his room, for, while being heartily against the arrangement, he could do nothing.

He brooded and planned a way out of the difficulty, only to find after much plotting and scheming that his plans were not workable.

To add to the old man's discomfort, the young officer was getting aggressive, for he read the French papers and noted, with uncon-

unconcealed pleasure, the predicament in which the Allles found themselves. He was not slow to assert that Germany would be victorious, that the Allies would bow to the Kaiser, and that France would be under the Prussian foot, and that the ground he was now domiciled on would be a German possession.

True to the Prussian type, the old man thought viciously, and with a tinge of bitterness.

Then a great idea came to him. He gave it serious thought. Why not have some of the Allied troops billeted in the chateau; it would keep the German underground, and maybe Nina might cast her eye on some other likely-looking lad. Papa Harmonger nursed the comforting thought until it became almost an obsession. Yes, he would do it-it might save Nina, his pride, his undying patriotism.

A call at headquarters of the 5th Army Corps and the matter was arranged. The Commandant would be pleased nay grateful, if Suret Harmonger would billet three officers and three men, and so it came about that three officers and three men were billeted in the chateau the next day. The womenfolk were apprehensive, but were assured that there was no danger if Karl kept to the cellar, and, he explained, it will help to allay any suspicion in the minds of our neighbours to have these soldiers billeted with us.

Then began an intrigue that was not to see its fulfilment until long after the dogs of war were once more lying dormant and peaceful.

Nina's visits to the hiding place of Karl became less frequent. Of necessity it behoved her to be careful, and these prolonged absences lay heavy on the ardent devotion of Karl.

One young officer attached to the chateau was obviously enamoured by Nina, and to his delight he found that Papa Harmonger looked not unkindly on his advances. Nay, the old man actually arranged and schemed out opportunities to bring them together.

He let it be known in the village that his daughter was much attached to a certain officer who was domiciled at the chateau, and so the news got around, as Papa Harmonger desired it would, for he knew that eventually the rumour would reach the ears of the old priest, who was the pivot point of all such gossip in the little village, and in due course Father Dupont would call on him for verification of the rumour.

In the course of a few days the good priest paid a visit to the chateau, and after refreshments and much verbal parrying, broached the subject of his errand.

"It is said in the village, good sir, that M'mselle Nina speaks of matrimony?"

"Marriage," Papa Harmonger echoed, "well, well," then as a flash of inspiration came to him, "Yes, that is so."

"My blessing on you, Pere Harmonger," the old cure said fervently. "It is good that it is so. A worthy girl, a worthy girl - a blessing in your old age, and, who knows a grandson for you and your good lady." He chuckled.

Little did the kindly priest know that unconsciously he had laid the foundation of a pretty little tragedy by his artless words.

"I am at your service, sir, at any time for the ceremony, and will be delighted - our oldest family - the prettiest girl in the village," and he rubbed his hands gleefully. "Good-bye," and with a hearty salutation he was gone.

For many weary days Papa Harmonger planned out a deep laid scheme, and one evening he called Nina to his room. "My child," he said, "I think you should be married. I have spoken to the good priest and I can arrange it."

Nina was speechless for a moment or two and then spoke.

"Oh, father, I am so happy. Karl" - the word hurt the old man - "will be so glad, if it could be arranged."

"You must not speak to him or see him until after the ceremony," her father spoke sternly. "It is desirable and necessary that it be not mentioned to anyone. I will arrange all the details; it will be necessary for him to be married in a uniform other than the one he is wearing. I will see to that. Be careful, child, lest by your actions my plans miscarry."

The deception will be complete, the old man mused, as he went upstairs to his room. There must be no mistake. It will be tomorrow night; yes, tomorrow would see the completion of his plans.

Early the next evening a party of officers were to be observed in the lounge of the chateau, having a royal time, singing, dancing, and sampling the best wines from the cellar, and at the host's invitation partaking much too liberally of whisky, rum, champagne and whatever drinks good Papa Harmonger could force on to them. As the night grew to a close, first one and then the other stumbled to their rooms; one lay under the table in a drunken sleep, another lay stretched out on the settee. Papa Harmonger's eyes were bright with suppressed excitement.

The old priest would be here at eleven o'clock, he must warn Nina to be in readiness; the plan must not go astray.

After an eternity of waiting and suspense, the priest arrived and was shown into the dimly-lit salon, the walls of which were adorned with pictures of past Harmongers, gay knights, great soldiers and fair women.

Nina came down the stairs, heavily veiled and timid, and from the open doorway of the lounge, the scene of the merry party, Papa Harmonger and an old servant supported between them the staggering figure of a soldier in a British uniform.

"He is ill and has been wounded," the old man assured the priest. "Let the ceremony begin."

It was a simple ceremony. Nina, timid and shy, whispered her acceptance of the man, and by judicious prodding and suggestions the khaki-clad figure mumbled the fateful words, "I will."

Nina turned to her lover, now her husband, and threw back her veil for the first caress. In the half light she peered into his face. "Mon Dieu," she screamed "it is not he!" And she dropped in a dead faint at his feet.

"Overwrought," the old cure murmured sympathetically, as he prepared to depart.

The soldier, the unconscious victim of this intrigue, straightened himself, looked into the face of the unconscious girl, then into the white, quivering face of Harmonger, and as his befuddled senses grasped the sorry mess he was in, turned and walked out of the open door into the night.

The central station at Paris was thronged with hurrying, bustling tourists, red-coated luggage porters dashed here and there, looking for prospective clients. The tang of glorious spring was in the air, happy parties stood in groups everywhere - everybody with that jolly holiday feeling breaking down all barriers, appeared to know everybody else. From the hurrying, happy throng one figure seemed to detach itself and stand out, vivid and mournful, as if oppressed with doubt and uncertainty. He spoke to no one, and seemed to be disinterested. A colonial, one would gather by his sun-tanned features, and the tall, lean frame, clear blue eyes and square, determined chin, and on closer observation one would say a soldier in those hectic days of war not long past, for across his forehead a livid scar showed clear and distinct - a searing bullet, a ball of shrapnel, or a fragment of high explosive shell, had made that scar.

He spoke to a porter - the train to Chantilly - and, handing the porter a note, he strolled up to the booking window.

Chantilly in spring is a never to be forgotten place. The weather is glorious, the surrounding country magnificent, the appointments of the hotels beyond reproach, and the entertainment on a lavish scale.

But it was for none of these attractions that the handsome young colonial went to Chantilly; it was to rest and try and recover his health.

An indulgent family, combined with the advice of an eminent specialist, had agreed on the necessity of a complete change and rest, for he was suffering from loss of memory, and the bullet that had nearly robbed him of his life had temporarily robbed him of his memory.

He took up residence in a quiet, refined hotel on the main thoroughfare, and to this day never regretted the choice.

It was on the second day of his stay in Chantilly that he was curiously attracted to the possessor of a remarkably good-looking face, and the possessor of that face was a slim slip of a young woman, with all the natural grace of her race, but with a far-away, almost disinterested outlook on life which appealed to the hand- some young stranger.

Introductions are scarcely necessary in post-war France, and it was inevitable that they soon became on speaking terms.

From the maid he learned. that her lover had been killed in the war. "M'sieur," the maid confided, "there is something greater that worries the little mademoiselle. What it is I do not know."

On the warm spring days they were often seen together on the promenade, or walking in the park, and to the observant watcher they both appeared to find a quickening interest in life, taking an interest in each other and in the things that interested either. The other quests of the hotel nudged each other slyly, and the old gossips forecasted an early engagement.

Then the handsome young man realised that he was in love with the pretty mam'zelle, and in a flash his memory was restored to him. He remembered he was married - a foolish jest, a stupid hoax doubtless, but nevertheless married. To whom he did not know.

The matter had gone too far for him to pack up and leave Chantilly, and beside, he was in love and he believed that m'zelle loved him in return. He would confess, throw himself on her mercy. She would understand, of that he was certain.

It was the night of the Ball Artiste, and after an intoxicatingly glorious waltz he led the dainty lady out into the moonlight across the lawn to a hidden snuggery, where he felt they would not be interrupted.

The sympathetic old moon who has mothered and sponsored many of these lovers' meetings, in many climes and among many people, had never looked down on a stranger romance than was to be enacted that night.

"You will sit down." The tall young man with the clear blue eyes and the determined chin bowed his fair partner to a seat. "I have some-

something very, very important to tell you. I do not know how to begin. You may condemn me, laugh at me. I will not blame you,"

Clearing his throat as though conscious of the importance of the occasion, he commenced:

"First I must confess my love for you. You are- are- you are everything to me. I dare not ask you to return that love for me. I am not worthy," he hastened to explain, "of your love. I am a beast, a rotten cad, although when I explain you may appreciate the position I was placed in."

The girl was weeping silently, He put his arms around her.

"I am married," he said tonelessly.

The girl gave a stifled sob and Mother Moon hid herself behind a vagrant cloud, a cold breeze swept across the lawn, and it seemed that this was the end of all things.

"I will tell you the story," he said. "It is not a pretty story, but all I ask when you have heard it is to forgive me.

"In 1917 I was a soldier, young in the ways of the world; left home to do my bit," he said simply, "and, like most of the other young fellows in my battalion, I liked a jolly time. Shortly after our arrival from Egypt and Gallipoli we were sent to a place here in France - I cannot remember the name of the village - and was billeted out to some very fine folk. I have tried to remember the name of the place, but I had a nasty wound. I - I sort of lost my memory, and it was in that village, when I was drunk, that someone played a stupid hoax on me. I got married," he said simply. "My brother officers told me that I was married, and the next day we went up to the front.

"I got this," and his hand went to his forehead. "I was bad for nearly two years. I was disgusted at my actions. It was only last night that I remembered about it. Will you forgive me?"

"Forgive you," her voice, to his ear, sounded far away. Somewhere he had heard that voice before.

"Forgive you," she said again, and then the calm reproach was levelled at him.

"Where did this happen?"

"I do not know."

"It would not be in 'Har' - her voice faltered; a piteous sob ended the words.

"Sweetheart," his arms were around her again, "I do not know."

The old moon, serene in her heavenly majesty may have given her cue, through the tall pines her gentle glow looked down on the two lovers.

He looked into her eyes, and, sensing with a true lovers's instinct a definite something that he could not define, repeated his answer, "I do not know."

A silence came over them - an indescribable silence, and then she spoke.

"My name," she said, "does not matter. I also am married. I was married one night in my father's chateau to a man whom I did not know. I saw him for a brief moment. It was a cruel jest. My lover, Karl, joined the Germans again after they had advanced. He was killed in 1918, in the Argonne zone - poor Karl!"

"Where did this happen," the man spoke quickly, almost passionately.

The answer came slowly, reverently: "At Harmonger, the Chateau of Harmonger, my father's place,"

A sibilant whisper stole through the pine trees, the moon shed her bright beams on the lovers.

"Nina," the man whispered, "it was you! My Nina, The Chateau Harmonger - my wife."

"Mon Dieu," the girl whispered as she put her arms around him. "It was you."

"It was me," whispered the man. "Thank God it was me - my Nina."

In a chateau on the borders of Belgium, you may, if you pass that way, see a pretty little madam tending the flowers, a small son is romping along the garden path, and a tall, handsome man watches them, with n smile in his blue eyes, a jest on his lips, as he calls to Nina to be careful.

In the shadows sits Mama Harmonger, with a smile of joy on her wrinkled old face.

Perchance, if you look in the window of the chateau when the sun is sinking you will see a bent, feeble old man, looking upwards to the pictures of his ancestors, and with a whimsical smile on his face, tell his faithful old servant that it is well.

The night is rich with the scent of honeysuckle, sweet jasmine and rose, the knowing old moon peeps in at the old-world garden, and smiles her knowing old smile; peace after storm, rest after labour.

THE GAME

Mud, dusk, and a somewhat limited panorama of Flanders! Flanders and mud we have come to look upon as one, and look on them as essential to the life of a soldier. Dusk we welcome; it giving us respite and rest for a few brief hours. Out in front, and behind us, a foggy mist rises from the ground, rising in weird, fantastic shapes as it strikes the upper air.

A slight breeze rustles the scanty foliage of a shattered tree to our left. It makes, to our ears, a hideous soul-searching cry for vengeance. When the star shells flare in mid-air it throws the tree out into weird relief, making it cast long, ragged shadows on. the ground. We think of the story that tree could tell if it could only speak. How it has seen the ebb and flow of battle; how nobly men fought; how they died; how they still die - defiant, to the end. Pointing with shattered arms to their goal, ever onward, up, Excelsior! as the old tree still points with the remains of its shattered trunk. Then it could tell yet another story; how the little children played beneath its sheltering branches; how they enjoyed the cool, refreshing shade cast by its thick foliage. Instead of deep scars in the ground, poppies and daisies and hundreds of other spring flowers adorned the surrounding landscape. How the nightingale made the night sweet with his hopeful melody. The nightingale still gives voice to his song; but it is more broken than before, and the trills, instead of a light-hearted hopefulness, take on a haunting, mournful sadness, with a touch of infinite longing for his old domain.

Far up in the sky a silver sheen shows for a moment and disappears. Suddenly the dark clouds are riven asunder and the old moon shines out in all her glory, casting a mellow, tender light over the torn and tortured ground around the trenches. It heartens us. We see, by this sign, some-thing bright and good to that which is before us. Taking advantage of the light of the moon, we peer towards our enemy. Big things are afoot tonight, and one slight slip might mean that some of our comrades will not answer the next roll call. But all is well. Intense silence; except at times, the spiteful, moaning hiss of a sniper's bullet; some- times a scream of agony.

"Everything ready?" the Corporal questions. "Got the bombs ready, Tommy?" Tommy, a big, hefty giant, answers "Yes!" Then, as an afterthought, he adds, "Corp., guess we'll give 'em the king hit tonight." Hardly are the words out of his mouth than the answer is given by a swishing roar above our heads. Bang! And what we have been waiting for has come.

The second shell comes from half right, rear. It is an isolated gun "feeling" for the rest of the battery. Another few moments of silence, then gl!ns all along the line take up the cannonade. The air is filled with a hurtling, swishing sound as the first salvo of shells speed on to their destination. We duck our heads with the shock of the firs1 explosion. In and out of the lesser bursting of the small shells we recognise the demoralising roar of the big sixty. pounders. These big shells plough up tons of earth, spread- ing death and destruction everywhere.

The roar of our shells gives us a feeling of security. We well know, by past experience, that "Fritz" will be keeping low. Perhaps he is even down in his dug-outs, some of them a considerable distance underground. Some of the men, taking a chance, risk a glance over the parapet to enjoy to the full, the sight of "Fritz's" discomfort. Those men who have not looked over get a fair inkling of how things go by the talk of the boys on the parapet. As the shells strike the earth sundry ejaculations are heard. "By hell, they are getting it hot now!" "Strike me pink, that was a beaut!"

Tommy, catching the spirit of the moment, fixes a grenade to his rifle, sardonically salutes it, and releases the trigger. He mounts the fire step in time to see where his bomb lands. "About five yards out," he mutters discontentedly; but, nevertheless, he seems to be highly pleased.

As he is getting the next grenade ready, his face creases up into a thousand wrinkles, he breaks into a broad, good-humoured grin. He sets his rifle at a more acute angle, kisses the grenade in grim sarcasm, and fires.

Our artillery is working itself into a pitch of fury before undreamed of, but we are used to the shriek and hiss of the shells by this; being more at home in action than silence and inaction. We glory in the red, raw hiss of the big shells as they hurtle on their way to destroy human life. "Out in front" "Fritz" has suddenly thought of something happening. Being too preoccupied gloating on "Fritz's" destruction we forget that he can retaliate. A sudden whiz, bang, thirty yards in front of us, makes us think more of safety and less of gloating.

The Corporal slides down from the fire-step and yells imperiously, "Keep in the parapet, boys; they will get the range next shot." And with a final injunction to our bomber, Tommy, "Tommy, you overgrown cow, cover. yourself up, will you?" Tommy expands his broad chest, his lovably, wicked face lights up with a wicked, scornful smile, be nevertheless he crouches into the parapet; not for his protection, but, as he says, "Lookin' safer; being orders, I must."

We all crouch close together. Somehow we feel safe at the thought, and the feel of warm, pulsating, human comradeship beside us, a comradeship before unheard of till the cry of the "War God" brought us together. "Brothers they were who found their brotherhood that night, and found it good."

A swift, sharp hiss, like the letting loose of a giant's pent-up fury, a dull thud, and we know the shell we have been waiting for has arrived. The second intervening between the thud and the burst cannot be explained. A second when the body is dead; yet every nerve and every thought twitch and become vivid and real; a second when the mind works quickly, turning every thought into a confused chaos of trepidation. It is a second that helps the body to withstand the shock that will follow. A second specially made for those in great danger. To be brief, the second between life and death.

Our small world of parapet, paradox and dug-out suddenly swells like a blister. Then, crash! A stomach-sickening crash, and the tension is broken. Mind reasserts itself over the body, and we are suddenly whisked back to the real.

"Who is hurt?" is the silent question asked in every mind. "Did you get it?" one man questions of a comrade, who is feeling himself all over. "Dunno," he answers, wondering if his answer is true or not. "Give us a look." After looking and seeing no sign of a wound he asks again. "Where do you feel it?" "Here an' here, an' here, an'--" "Hold on laddie, don't be silly; that was some lumps of dirt 'it yer." "Hell! I forgot; thort I was knocked a treat." "Well, I dunno what you'll think when a lump does 'it yer and knocks yer rotten. Guess you'll think all Krupp's iron foundry suddenly 'it yer under the chin," the good Samaritan mumbles cheerfully, as he moves off to help some less fortunate comrade.

The Corporal, missing Tommy, asks, quickly, "Where's that silly cow gone to now?" His looks do not speak his inner-most thoughts; his face betrays a look of troubled concern. He does not mean anything when he calls Tommy a "silly cow." If nobody had been listening he would have said, "Where's that dear old comrade of mine?" As language such as dear, and comrade, do not sound well in out primeval surroundings, a veneer of slang is generally used. The worse the name the better the man.

Tommy is soon found underneath some fallen sand bags, is none the worse for his imprisonment, and, after a drink of water, curses the Germans for fully five minutes. "What. are you swearing at, Tommy? Anyone would think that you had been half killed." "That's what's making me swear, to think that I should get such a 'ell of a fright and not get a wound, so's I could get a trip to 'ospital for awhile. Ain't it rotten?" he asks of nobody in particular.

We agree with him. It certainly is a bit hard.

This little excitement over, we start to build up our shattered parapets, preparing for the shrapnel that will fol low the high explosives. We know the high explosive shells ire meant to dislodge us, and once dislodged, then the shrapnel takes a heavy toll of victims. We build our parapets up, bag for bag, hand over head, and then settle down to waiting. The hardest of the lot. The order: "Fix bayonets: first whistle, mount fire step; second whistle, charge!" is passed along to us from the commanding officer further up the line. "Make no noise!" is the final order.

"Make no noise!" No noise in this fearful din. Unconsciously we speak in whispers. Although the order is funny to an extreme it has to be obeyed. The order incessantly flits through the brain, "Make no noise!" You feel as if you want to tell everybody, with the result, if a shell makes sound a little bit out of the ordinary you jump unknowingly.

A sudden whipping and crackling in the air above us, and we know the shrapnel shells are coming over. The Corporal gives the very unuecessary command. "Down!" But we are down long before the order formed on his lips, for we well know the result of standing up while shrapnel is whizzing through the air. One chap went back to hospital with a piece in his head yesterday.

At last we hear the short, sharp bark of our trench mortars, followed by a rumbling snarl as they strike the wind. Men clutch their rifles closer to them. It is a little comfort to feel the sleek, smooth woodwork of the rifle. It is a true friend! The shells are coming over in hundreds, and we know that every field piece from the smallest to the largest is working overtime.

Again we get the order, "Fix bayonets!" This order is the height of a soldier's ambition. What we have been trained up to is to take this order. "Fix bayonets!" calmly and as a matter of course. This is the moment men have waited for since enlisting. How many men have tried to picture this moment when training on. the sands of Egypt! It could be fittingly described as the climax of a soldier's life. What will follow in the next half-hour is what the soldier has been trained to; and that, in a nutshell, is to kill as quickly as possible, and, at the same time, to be careful of his own life; Is it any wonder men's hands tremble and shake as they fix the bayonets to their rifles! Soldiers have been described in the doing of that act as bloodthirsty; but it is hardly so. Is a prospector, who, after searching for gold for twelve months, finds his heart's desire, greedy! Is a soldier to be described as bloodthirsty when he cries for vengeance for helpless women and babes, who have been foully murdered? No. So we fix bayonets and get slightly hot in the head in the doing of it. The heat in the head gradually develops into an all-consuming flame, scorching and searing refinement, until we emerge different men. Supermen! with the lust to kill; the lust to kill those who have killed without cause; they who have murdered women, outraged children, and slaughtered old men, for lust only - not for any military achievement.

The crashing and banging of the shells make us half delirious and incapable of thinking properly. Someone tries to raise a laugh, but fails miserably. Every man is listening to the hissing, moaning wail of the shells, interspersed with demoralising crashes. It pulsates and throbs through the brain till it takes on an unearthly scream that seems to say, "Kill or be killed! Kill or be killed ! ! Kill or--"

A cry of "Ten men, stretcher-bearers! Ten men, stretcher-bearers!" helps us to gain control over our wandering thoughts. Still the cry goes on -"Ten men, stretcher-bearers! Ten men, stretcher--" A sharp hiss, a crash, and we find ourselves repeating the sentence that will never be finished in this world -"Ten men, stretcher-bearers! Ten men. stretcher-bearers !"

A shell whizzes just over oar heads and fails to explode. "A dud," the Corporal jerks oat, his voice sounding odd and out of place. We laugh - a shrill, mirthless laugh that in ordinary times could never come from men; a laugh full of ironical satire, sounding unearthly and unreal.

Again the order comes, "Five minutes; no noise! Section commanders, keep the men in proper alignment!"

The roar and din of the shells suddenly abates. From far behind our lines we hear the sweet music of the church bells, calling the very old and the very young to early morning mass. What memories those bells bring back! The time when we went to church; when we were classed as "good" boys by the people of the town: how we used to say our prayers. But all is well; we are still all right. Instead of prayer we fight - fight for religion! Prayers are useless when not backed up by a firm resolve. Two strong arms and spirit are worth a thousand prayers when the War God is stalking through the land feeding on men's blood. Thousands of such thoughts flit and pass through our minds like so many shadows. At the consoling sound of the bells Tommy begins to hum a sarcastic ditty:

"Take me over the sea, where the Germans can't snipe at me;
Oh, my! I don't want to die, I want to go home--"

The Corporal is putting the final words to a much-begrimed letter of farewell to his loved one. It has been in his pocket for months awaiting this moment. "Good-bye, good luck, don't worry!" he unconsciously murmurs as he writes. "Good-bye, good luck, don't worry!" It keeps repeating in our minds.. The Corporal looks strangely wan and worried as he replaces the letter in his pocket.

Tommy asks of a comrade, "'Ave you said 'Good-bye, good luck,' laddie?" The answer comes brief and to the point, "Nope; ain't goin' to be 'sloughed' ter-day."' "How der yer know?" "Dunno; something seems ter tell me my luck's in." Then, as if not quite certain, "Hope so anyway." "That's right, crack hardy. Why, yer might git flowers on yer grave if yer luck's in. Yer might. Luck's a fortune!" "Yes; luck's a fortune all right," answers the man, his face twisting up into a devil-may-care grin.

From a little to the left a signal is given. "Pheet"- the signal for us to mount the fire-step. Another minute and we will be out in that strip of land falsely named "No Man's Land!" Another minute before we know our fate! What a long lime it seems - hours, days, years. "Pheet." We crawl and slide over the parapet, the Corporal taking the lead and givmg us pace. "Keep back!" he hisses, through tightly closed teeth, to a man who stumbles over a piece of barb wire.

We advance stealthily, silently, truly; grim men with a grim duty. Every man keeps in line as though on parade. For a mile each side of us our comrades are doing the same. Men stumble into old shell holes, recover themselves and press steadily on, with never a sound. Much depends on our silence. If we are heard approaching, before we get anywhere near them - well, the game is up! The Germans, knowing full well our trenches will be packed to overflowing, waiting for the moment when we will need reinforcements, will deal with us, and then turn their field pieces on to the trenches we have just vacated. We have to be careful!

Hardly are we on to his barb wire, than we are seen. A sudden, sharp signal from the enemy's trench, and then "Swish. swish, swish!" Two men go down with the first stream of lead. Lucky they are firing high! The next man to go down is our Corporal. He clasps his hand to his head, half turns in his stride, and drops. We know he is mortally wounded, but cannot stop to help him.

Tommy darts ahead into the Corporal's place, yelling as he does. "By hell, boys, we want the first dozen we come across for that!" As if for answer bayonets are lowered, gleaming wicked and sinister in the early morning light. All caution is thrown to the winds now we know we are seen.

"Right!" Tommy yells, as he breaks into a run. A long line of evil-looking men, with bodies crouched as if for a spring and with bayonets lowered sweeps after him.

What follows is hidden by a red mist before the eyes. All you know is that you are amongst the Germans - amongst the enemy; to kill him; if not to kill him to be killed yourself. Ten minutes, maybe an hour, before you regain your normal senses. No enmity is felt for the dead Germans in the trench. They fought well; we fought better. A badly wounded German asks for a drink of water, or something to that effect. He is given a drink, and then disarmed.

High up in the heavens we hear the droning buzz of an aeroplane. We look up to see if it is one of ours or "Fritz's." At last we catch a glimpse of it outlined against the morning sun.

Away up there it looks a mere speck. It is behind our lines, making towards us, so we surmise it is ours. It is nearly overhead before we see the red, white and blue emblem on the under part of its wings.

It is cheering to see it sail along so calmly, sedately. It may also give our artillery some targets to fire at. We hope so. It will give us a little respite. The enemy are sure to answer our guns if they begin to "feel" for his batteries. It will relieve the strain on the trenches and may even develop into an artillery duel.

The 'plane is barely half way over "No Man's Land" before the enemy's "Archies" are flinging shells at it. The light anti-aircraft shells make a musical sound as they soar towards the heavens - like a deep bass and a shrill treble intermingled into a musical one.

The 'plane dives, rises, slides over, and rights itself. We marvel how it escapes, but steady eyes and steady nerves are guiding it on its way. We are. not the only ones in danger, and that fact, somehow, seems to give us a feeling of security. At last we see one, two, three smoke balls drop from the aeroplane. The men up there watching have discovered an enemy battery and are giving its position away to our gunners.

Tommy hands around his water bottle. We drink sparingly by wetting our lips and tongues, and passing it on, We have not got too much water, and if the enemy keep up the barrage much longer somebody will have to attempt to get back to our second line and get some, and that will mean almost certain death. After replacing his water bottle, Tommy begins to feel through his pockets. After a lot of hunting and turning out of pockets, he reveals the object of his search - a cigarette butt and some matches. He lights the precious portion of cigarette. Every man, as if obeying an order, puts down his rifle and watches the owner of the "butt." We watch him greedily, our mouths moist with anticipation. He takes a long draw, gulping the soothing smoke well back into his lungs; holding it there as if loath to part with it.

One of the hungry ones begins to ransack his tunic pockets. He knows full well there are no cigarettes there, but it is some consolation to search for one. He goes through his pockets slowly, methodically; his hands trembling. He may find a butt; one never knows. His face suddenly lights up like a man who has made a startling discovery. We hold our breath as he disengages his hand from his pocket. At last we see what he has found - a ten shilling note. He looks at it in his hand, this note; this sign of wealth.

Our faces drop. What can money buy here? What is the use of money when duty, expectant comrades, require you to produce something better, even if it be a cigarette? What can money buy? Fame? with the loss of honour. Is money to be a substitute for a cigarette? Is it any wonder one man sneers with scorn, and yet cannot tell why it has affected him so!

Up on the fire-step, Tommy lounges, his feet moving lazily to and fro, his eyes half closed. We could kill him for his idle content. "Here, Tommy, I'll give you this half quid for a draw." Tom closes his eyes and leans back, opening his eyes again to expel a cloud of smoke from his lungs.

This is worse torture than shell fire. We smell the faint, haunting fragrance of the precious weed; it bites deep into our vitals. "Tommy, I'll give yer this half quid for a draw," in piteous tones from the "moneyed man."

Tommy takes another draw, then taking the cigarette lovingly from between his teeth, straightens up and asks quietly, "Do yer think I'm after blood money, boy? Stick that half quid in yer kick and have a go at this. Give 'em all a go at it, it's theirs as much as mine." And Tommy-big, wicked-looking white-hearted Tommy - begins to oil his rifle in preparation for the next "stunt."

The artillery have suddenly got tired of what they have been doing - destroying human life. We sit back for awhile. Some are drowsy. After the strenuous work of the last few days everybody is more or less a little fanciful. One man mentions Australia! Several men get up and move about aimlessly. We do not want to awake the old longing for our native land. But we have lost our Corporal, and we feel a little bit sentimental, so we gather together and talk.

One man takes us back to Australia by his talk of the last walk he had with his sweetheart. Nobody laughs. We have all been through the same, if not with sweetheart, a mother. Someone asks, "Is she a dinkum tart?" The answer comes, dreary and far away, "Yes, dinkum." We let it go at that. We talk of our homes, our hopes, our ambitions.

A young farmer begins to tell us his dory. A story of a greater, more silent battle than the one we are now in. A story of hardship, work and privation. He carries our minds vividly back to Australia by his talk of the great Australian bush. He takes our minds away from the blood-soaked trenches and transplants them on a hill overlooking his homestead.

He musters his sheep for our inspection; shows us his cattle, his ploughed land. He points out where the great bush fire swept through. The next year a drought. He shows us the skeletons of his animals. Now, when it is too late, as if in mockery, long sprouts of grass grow around them. "Even the rabbits died that year," he tells us. We see old Dobbin, the horse who is getting lazy - fat for want of work.

We go to the gully at the back of the house. The sun is sinking. As it sinks lower it turns the green of the trees to darker green, from darker green to a thousand and one shades of amber. The highest peaks of this, Nature's own castle, stand out in vivid relief as the sun dips behind them. A little way up the gully a little brown rabbit peeps timidly out of its burrow. The silence giving it courage, it comes out to feed on the fresh, young undergrowth. From away up on the hill comes the voice of the lyre bird as he parades himself, full of vanity and love-making.

As we have had enough of sight-seeing for the time being, we move back to the homestead for tea. In fancy we partake of the good things - brown bread, cream cakes, and butter. After tea we sit around the fire. Two little children come to kiss their father good night. "Good night! Nanny, Jack." "Good night, dad, and Gawd' bless you!"

The clock on the mantelpiece strikes the hour of eleven. Everything is at rest outside. In the big gum by the side of the house, a native bear cries out - a human, pathetic cry, full of sympathy and sorrow. A mopoke's call rings out, dull and monotonous. A moth batters its wings against the lamp glass. Attractive things are always dangerous. Soon the place is in darkness. A mischievous 'possum scampers over the stable roof; the horses stop their contented munching for a moment and then continue.

Away out here on the hill lies rest. A cock crows from the hen roost; the fowls preen their wings.

Morning is breaking, a calm, peaceful morn, heralded in by the musical lay of the magpie, A laughing jackass gives voice to his cheerful song. The smaller birds wake to life, and soon the sweet, fresh air throbs with their unaffected music. An old man kangaroo in the crop paddock pricks up his ears, and questions of the air. He hops off in huge bounds, clearing the wire fence in his stride. A slight breeze rustles the foliage of the big gums. Our gums! It makes a sound as of running water. A merry, dancing, little stream, bubbling and gushing with joy.

So life in the trenches goes on. Where is the soldier who would not have these times back again? Good times for a great purpose!.

THE UNKNOWN

Behind the little hill where I was standing a military band played a stirring march. The music ended and out of the silence came the sad sweet notes of a bugle sounding that mournful dirge for sleeping heroes, "The Last Post."

I bared my head in mute respect to a hero and stood to attention until the melancholy wistful notes died fitfully away.

Then I looked down into Sausage Gully that lay below me, where groups of cold white crosses showed out vividly against the red of the poppies and the green bush on the adjoining hillside. A faint perfume of lilac and honey-suckle tingled my nostrils, and from a nearby farmhouse came the mellow bleating of a calf calling for its mother - the raucous quacking of ducks - and the merry twitter of birds sheltering in the newly-growing hedge.

Over near the old Poiziers road a little group of pilgrims came slowly into view, and wended their way down into the gully to the white crosses that sprinkled the floor of the valley.

They walked slowly, reverently, as though aware that they were treading sacred ground - and now and again someone would step from the party and pause before a grave - as if in deep thought, and then walk slowly on. These little white crosses marked the resting place of the gallant attackers of 1916 - boys who had flung themselves into the jaws of death, while yet still in the first flush of manhood - radiant with youth and vitality - fearing death as only youth can fear it - yet not afraid to die for comrades, country and the home folk.

The crosses clustered together more thickly on the crest of a little knoll at the far end of the valley, and the pilgrims marched down the narrow aisle two by two. Many there were who supported a feeble old man or woman-sturdy veterans who had fought on this historic spot in the past years, returning with their aged parents, or the parents of their late comrades, to pay homage to their dead. A sad wistful sight it presented, now all peace and quietness, with only the grim mocking crosses to disturb the quiet rustic beauty of the spot.

A few short years ago - the devil himself ran amok in this quiet sylvan retreat - death swift and terrible, silently and mercifully instant, rained from the high heavens and from the very bowels of the earth. Men staggered around here with blood lust in their very souls, wounds in their bodies, and a curse or a prayer on their lips, as they hacked and tore their way forward into the very jaws of death and eternity. Not only are their bodies buried there, but also the hearts of their mothers and fathers - the radiant love of a young sweetheart, the beauty of life, the poetry of ambition - all ruined and dead at one fell sweep of the War God's sword.

I sighed deeply and gazed into the valley below me. Down among the little white sentinels an old aged mother lifted her bowed head to the blue sky above. The tears streaked her care-worn face, and half stifled sobs shook her feeble body.

A slim young girl in white with a red poppy at her breast knelt at the foot of the same grave. She rose to her feet and held out her arms as if imploring the old lady to comfort her - with a pitiful little cry the girl nestled into welcoming embrace of those tired old arms and buried her head in that bosom which had also nestled there her soldier son before whose grave they now stood. Mother and daughter may be, or mother and young wife - who can tell. I brushed the mist that was dimming my eyes impatiently away, and turned to gaze to the east, where the sun would rise tomorrow, giving a new hope and new encouragement to the world and to people so sorely stricken as this.

Another bugle call roused me from my reverie, clear and distinct it sounded in the faint afternoon breeze, and it recalled my attention to the scene before me.

The call was "attention," and I stood there and watched the impressive ceremony.

Down the aisle marched a body of men, some with sleeves flapping in the wind, others on crutches with their empty trouser flaps beating a tattoo against their supports, others were being led - the scarred veterans of this field come back to honour their glorious dead.

Silently and impressively the little group halted before the cluster of crosses. The old lady and the girl were tenderly led aside.

The firing party took up their position, the rifles in the hands of the veterans snapped to "Present."

A padre stepped out of the ranks and spoke a few words in a low, hushed, yet impressive voice; then he too stepped aside. Then came a rattle of rifles as the group raised their rifles to their shoulders. An order was given and with a crash that echoed and re-echoed within the valley the rifles fired a volley across the graves of those sleeping heroes. Again the rifles crashed out, then the group grounded their butts on the grass and silently uncovered before their dead. Again the wistful strains of "The Last Post" rang out wailing away into the distance like the cry of a doomed soul in the valley of the shadow. The evening shadows lengthened, a warm glow lit up the western sky, the scent of jasmine and honeysuckle made the cool air fragrant - the little calf was silent, the birds had ceased their chattering and a distant church bell tolled the evening hour. I turned sadly away from this scene of bitterness and strife, of peace and sleep, and gazed longingly into the eastern sky - trusting and confident of a better day to come.

GOODBYE SUSETTE

The days I spent in that quiet little village will remain a treasured memory to me. Susette and I tended the graves carefully, and roamed care-free over the countryside. We would sup at some little way-side inn and return in the evening, hand in hand, with contentment in our hearts and the surge of a new-found joy in our breasts. She was a wonderful creature, this Susette; the sweetness of her, the sympathy and understanding, made her all too lovable. At times I felt anxious for her. Even now I can see her plucking weeds from the graves, her bright eyes wet with tears as she thought of the mothers and sweethearts who loved that boy sleeping there in his shallow grave.

"Susette," I would say, "are you unhappy? Why, little girl, do you shed those tears?"

Her red lips would part, and she would smile and say, "Ami, I am happy, so happy, here among your countrymen, and yet my heart is sad; my tears are not for myself, but the consoling tears of all women who mourn their dead. Kiss me, Ami, for you are a strong man and do not understand a woman's tears. It is not sadness or pain that we women cry for; a mother cries over her baby, sheds unseen tears for him when he is a big man like you, Ami, and cries more when he is lowered into the grave. And would you have it different? You strong men face the result with unflinching eye and brave heart; you die with a laugh, that is how we like you to die - and your last thought is of her who gave you life. We, M'sieur, the mothers of men, give life; we cannot put our backs to the wall and take it - unless - unless we are greatly wronged. It is our desire, when great issues are at stake, but not our nature, and so, ever so quietly, we go to some forgotten corner, if the odds are against us, and die. It is good that it is so, for, Ami, the weak look to the strong, and the strong protect the weak. You would not have us like wild cats, who fight with tooth and claw. The strength of man is our inspiration, his chivalry and devotion is our shrine. You love the weakness and softness, and so we worship one the other, and that is the cycle of life. You could kill us with one ounce of your strength, yet we rule you and command you, for we, Ami, are the life-givers and the mates of men."

Her eyes were sparkling, her lips moist. I felt, or thought I felt, as I looked at her, the cry of suffering humanity ringing down the corridors of time, until it pierced my heart - the single tear of a good woman seemed to drench the world in sweetness and anguish. I seized her by the shoulders. She was the spirit incarnate, this frail little creature was life. Those eyes spoke of heaven, and I her man, stood revealed to her. the passion and dross that was me turned to clay, and there we stood, Life and Death, she frail and eternal, I big, but a shell. I felt the clammy earth around me, and heard a mournful dirge as; they lowered me down. Her warm lips on mine broke the spell. I heard her say, "Ami, you are crying too: why, what is wrong? You great big boy...." Great sobs shook my body and the unwilling tears coursed down my checks. She – this God-given treasure -mothered me and soothed me, whispered silly little thing to me, stroked my hair, and nestled my head to her bosom, and 1 was comforted.

I spoke my heart to her that bright afternoon, for I felt, after the recent tears, that she was mine, hut the more I cajoled, fretted and begged, the more she resisted me, and eventually refused me her lips. Her dear eyes were cold and hard, her lips drawn tight, her hands clenched. She looked an old woman.

I pleaded as if for life. I did not understand - or will I ever understand? As we turned a bend in the road she stopped; her eyes were fixed. "Cherie!" I said, becoming more alarmed, what it is – what is wrong?"

"M'sieur." She said, and only her lips moved, "can you see that house?" That was all she said. My heart froze within me. I followed the direction of her gaze, for I knew then - La Mort - my Susette, with blood on her hands. I turned to protest with her, but she anticipated me and said "Come!" I followed, with bowed head and aching heart, praying the while to my God to help her and me. She led me on, into the grounds of La Mort, and pointed out a tiny mound.

With heaving bosom and clenched hands, she confronted me. "Ami," she said, and her voice was broken, "that - and she pointed to the grave - was mine and theirs.... My baby," she sobbed - Ami, forget me -"kiss me once more, and then you must go, for ever."

Out of the sweetness of her kiss hate and sorrow were born; it was a kiss of dry ashes. A hatred for the great wrong sustained, consumed me; sorrow because I could not share it with her. I was willing, but her natural refinement was a barrier between us, and we parted in the grounds of La Mort for ever, I to a life of loneliness, she to the same.

Thousands of miles separate us now. but God gave dreams and God has helped me to believe La Mort was but a dream.

TAKE ME-GIVE ME!

Take me back to distant Flanders,
To the "billet" on the hill,
Put me back in front line trenches,
Put me there - but not to kill.
Give me back my dear old "cobbers,"
Give me back my good old gun,
Give me back the evening shadows -
Evenings that we spent in fun.

Give to me the dish of "bully,"
Give to me the soothing "fag";
The time we spent in Bacchus worship,
When every man was termed a "dag."

Give me back the chaffing banter
Of good comrades, tried and true,
They who taught, in days of darkness,
That the sky is ever blue.

Let me taste the cheering biere,
Let me sip the warming "vin,"
Let me have an Army biscuit,
Let me hear the battle's din.

THE ETERNAL SILENCE

Yes, I would put on my uniform today and go up to the front line and find the old, familiar landmarks I told Madam of what I intended to do, and she was delighted. She would be off to the village if M'sieur had no objections to get her vegetables, as they were very scarce yet, and the early buyer had a greater variety to choose from, and would M'sieur mind if tonight she gave a little party in honor of his return and invite a few Mamzelles, with bright eyes and red lips to remind him that after all France was France, and Madam still remembered Monsieur's failing for the company of sweet Mamzelles. Yes, M'sieur was quite agreeable; in fact, he thought it an excellent idea, looking at it in whichever light you please. Madam left me, flushed and rougish looking. I proceeded with my dressing, and must say I did credit to my native land, for I was trimly built and my uniform was nicely pressed.

Lighting a cigarette, I strolled outside and soon became the centre of an admiring group of villagers, who greeted me with delighted surprise, for, as I expected, my uniform was my passport to their hearts, and they who saw me told others that an Australian soldier had arrived in the village. I greeted many whom I remembered; the old cure, with his snow-white hair, blessed me, and haggard old dames, with scanty hair and cold, fearless eyes, warmed me, for we Australians could cut more wood and draw more water in one hour than they could from dawn to sunset, and it takes an old lady remember a little kindness like that. I stepped out bravely and with a feeling of great pride. They had made me their king for the time being, not for myself, but for the country my uniform represented. I was soon in the open fields. The ground is still serried and pock-marked with shell holes, and the reserve trenches were overgrown with weeds, and tall, lank grass. So I went on to the second and first line of resistance, pausing now and again to let my mind roam at will over many memories. That dug-out to my left was my home for three desperate days. There, alongside of it, is a grave. I know it well. It was I who scooped the cavity with my entrenching tool, and sent a prayer to Heaven for the soul of the lad who went before. I went across No-man's-Land, over and beyond the once German trenches. Once we fought for months to gain this strip of country; now it is useless. A strange, sinister silence broods over it, an uncanny feeling grips you. You long for the sound of cannon again, not because you like it, but because the silence does not seem real, and by the noise we knew it.

Retracing my steps, I went to a field a little way from the road, across a small creek, and on until I discovered the object of my search - a little cross with these words on it: "Our Darling Mamzelle, Her Comrade and Ours." I tended the grave carefully. A big, rough Digger lay beneath, and in his dead arms he clasped a little figure in a pitiful little white nightdress, stained with their blood. You remember how they died - he tried to save her and they were both struck down; and so we found them and buried them. No, it does not seem so long ago since she called the dead men the naughty men, for leaving her without saying good-bye, and laughed with delight to see a sorely-wounded man make faces for her to laugh at. Dear little soul, I thought, as I plucked a weed from the head of the grave, what unborn knowledge and sorrow you carried into that mound of earth. And the big soldier lying there with her, clasping her for protection: so he would take her across the valley of the shadow to her home. Dear little Mamzelle, what joy and comfort you brought the weary soldier, who, thousands of miles away from his own land, stroked and kissed her pretty hair and baby face, and so you lie with the sleeping-men, in the land of sorrow and beauty, where mothers' hearts and thoughts are hovering over your grave today, for France is not a strange country to them, but a memory of good sons and brave gentlemen, and so we leave you sleep, little girl, in your comrade's arms. I bared my head to the memory of the grief-stricken mother who mourned with us that day - they were buried - and to the rough soldiers who sobbed, unashamed, as the earth was heaped upon them. In fancy I kissed her baby lips again, and told her not to be afraid - we were there to stop the

Germans! All things must end, and so I left them, sadly, and with many a backward glance, for it is one thing to see a soldier die on the field of battle and another to see a sweet child mangled by enemy guns.

I passed many familiar places on my way home to the village, and dotted here and there are the little crosses that mark the dead, for this is the land of dead men and wistful dreams, and many of those crosses reared their heads not above soldiers, but dear pals of mine. My heart was heavy and my spirit dulled. I felt a wistful desire to be with them; voices seemed to call me and greet me. The sweet-smelling country-side and the bright sun spoke of peace, quiet, restful peace. I communed with their spirits and wended my way home, and, tramp, tramp, tramp, the phantom army followed me, all in perfect unison, for my heart rested with them, and I - I understood.

THE CURSE OF THE BRUTE

Rolling and billowing like the mountain mists in the grip of a tempest, the green-coloured clouds roll on, enveloping the landscape and blotting out the horizon. Silently, grimly, the vile thing creeps on, stretching out ever and anon, insidious little tentacles to grasp what life remains and throttle it, "Gas!" At the dread cry the villagers flee before the approaching danger, leaving the sick and halt to suffer strangulation, and, passing over it, leaves death, stark and horrible, for the innocent victims of Kultur.

They were writhing in the death-agony, trying to tear their throats out. It was awful. They were cursing God for being allowed to live.

I have never witnessed a more pathetic sight; it was heart-rending to see those magnificent men blinded, and with the flesh blistering off their bones. This new German invention, the flame-thrower, is a creation of the devil - it is not war.

It was proved beyond dispute that ten young girls of the village had been captured and maltreated, first by the officers and then by the German soldiery. Their bodies were found in the manure heap, close to where they met their death. One of them had her breasts cut off; another had been disembowelled, presumably with a bayonet.

On the wall of a house in Lille you could yet see the mark where an infant's head had been smashed in a fury of hate. The young mother was killed by a rifle butt.

One institution in France houses nearly 1000 girls, now raving lunatics, due to ill-treatment at the hands of the Hun.

The old people who could not march were herded together in the village square and shot, their bodies being left unburied for days.

At Ypres a Canadian soldier was found nailed to the door of a barn. There was indisputable evidence that be had been crucified while alive.

The advancing Germans were seen bayoneting the wounded lying on the ground.

In an underground factory we found a German boiling-down works, and the dead were taken here and thrown into high vats; then the ghouls boiled the bodies down to recover the fat.

A typical instance of Hun Kultur was witnessed on the front yesterday. A party of stretcher-bearers working under the white flag were fired on; they were all killed. Then the German snipers practised on the bodies. When recovered the bodies were riddled with bullets.

When our troops connected with the Germans and got amongst them with the bayonet they threw up their hands and cried "Kamerad! Kamerad!"

They came across No Man's Land in droves, with their hands up, crying, "Mercy, kamerad!" The Hun certainly is no good when the tables are turned. The only piece of work he has done thoroughly yet is spoilation and the ill-treatment of helpless women.

Docile, and peering timidly from behind big spectacles, the German delegate arrived for the Peace Conference. They agreed to everything - a true indication that the Hun admitted defeat.

Germany refuses to pay the indemnity. Today French and German troops clashed on the occupied territory.

The night life of Berlin is a revelation. Paris and New York pale into insignificance before it.

It was lunch time at a big German factory in Stettin. Two erstwhile soldiers of the Fatherland were talking about the war. "Mein Gott," said Fritz, "what a great time we had. Remember those twenty little French girla at --, and that dog of a colonial soldier at Ypres; he didn't like the idea of getting the nails through his hands and feet at all, did he?" Carl laughed at the happy memory. "But, Fritz, my boy," said he, "you forgot that poor, idiotic stretcher-bearer at Armentiers. Didn't we give it to him. I must have put half a dozen bullets into him myself. Remember the next day we were captured. 'Kamerad, kamerad, Gott straff the Hunds.' It tasted like poison to say it, but it was safer, Fritz; they were Australians." "Australians, eh?" Well, that's too good. Here we are making that consignment of toys for the young Australians - the foreman told me this morning. "Ha! Ha! Ha!" And they both laughed merrily. "The curse of the Fatherland be on the brats," said Fritz viciously. "Yes," said Carl, "Deutchcr ubes Alles. Who said Germany never won the war?"

And here I sit, an old man, mixing with phantom shapes and wistful dreams. They . . . They will find me in the morning—dead.

GOODBYE

My stay in France was all too brief. The gaiety and life of Paris grows on one, and you leave it with genuine feelings of regret, and with the resolve that some day you will return to the wonderful city. There are so many types of people, such a varied collection of characters, so many different amusements to engage your attention and please the mind, that in leaving it you feel as if you are parting with something that has unconsciously become part of you, and an experience that you will always have pleasant recollections of. A little group of acquaintances bade me Godspeed at the quay. Even my old landlady was there to bid M'sieur Australian good-bye and good luck. It was hard to part from such good friends, hut there was one consolation to relieve the feeling of despondency that gripped me, and that was, I was returning home. Home to the wanderer is a very real thing, goal to strive for, a beacon lighting the way.

  I arrived in England late that afternoon, and stopped at a modest hotel near the wharf. The next day I visited Harefield Park, and renewed old friends there. Harefield is rich in memory of the Australian soldier, for here the battered men arrived from the battlefields, and spent their convalescence in ideal surroundings. Many Diggers will remember the Old White Horse Inn at Harefield. It was out of bounds when the majority of us knew it, but today it is within bounds, and a jocular, fat-paunched proprietor still serves the light dinner ale, so dear to the heart of the convalescing Digger, but I doubt if it tasted as good when you can go into the bar without fear of being caught, and drink at your leisure, and know that there is no officious military policeman outside to make you account for your sins. I carried many messages from Harefield to Diggers in all parts of Australia, from the Gulf to Perth, and to give an idea how easy it would be to find an erring Lothario, I was given names, such as Smith and Brown, and

Private Digger who owned Prince's Bridge Station, and whose father was very rich, and owned the big Yarra Bank in Melbourne. Sergeant Blank, I was informed by one sweet young maid, lived in a big mansion at Melbourne. On enquiring where the place was, I was shown a photo. of Parliament House, and assured that he and his forefathers had lived there since the time of Captain Cook, and if I would call and give Sergeant Blank the little lady's undying love she would be delighted. Of course, I myself was taking a trip on the results of my huge wool cheque. One thing I was certain of, the Australian will never be forgotten in the places where he congregated in any number. Every man was a wealthy citizen in that wonderful country, Australia, and is there any wonder, considering the impression the Digger made with the little money at his disposal, for he scattered it indiscriminately for a few hours, and retired into dignified seclusion until the next pay came along, and, by so doing, he retained his reputation and status as a wasteful millionaire. even if it was only for a few hours. After all, it was worth-while. It is good to think that you have a good reputation in another part of the world, even if your own cheque would not be accepted for sixpence in your own country.

Horseferry Road is deserted, and no one misses the Digger more than the small shopkeepers in this district. Life for them has no spice now, business is slack, and the ending of the war for them was a thing for regret, for never before nor since have they seen money spent so grandly or freely. For one pound sterling I was offered a stylish pair of trousers, a silk tussore shirt, and a tunic that in war-time would command anything around the region of ten pounds. But that class of wearing apparel is at a discount now, and so I left them, much to the regret of the anxious seller.

The shores of old England arc fading from sight; on the starboard we catch now and again the twinkling light along the French beaches. "Good-bye Susette," I call, "Good-bye, Madam." The rushing wind snatches the words from my mouth, and in fancy I hear them call, "Adieu, Mon Brave, Bon Sonte."

RUMINATIONS

"Cheering multitudes flocked to Amiens from the whole of the Somme to pay a tribute to their Australian saviours."

In the depths of my drawer lay my badge - a little disc of brass that for many, many months I had not worn. It lay snug in its bed of wadding, a bauble scorned, and overlooked, its value priced in blood and valour, wounds and death, unprocurable and practically valueless, reckoned in coin of the realm, yet in the hard bitter struggle for existence it had been forgotten in a semi-conscious sort of way, for with it fixed on the lapel of your coat you become a poor devil, to be sympathised with and pitied, and tolerated, consequently with good red blood coursing the veins the badge of sacrifice had to suffer (one was made to feel as though it was the hallmark of folly.

Dark, sad days in Flanders were forgotten; long, long nights of bitter struggle and horror with death at your elbow, for companion, striking ever and anon some valiant soul, who for a space flaunted him and his ghastly mission, retreat and advance; the imps of bell emptying vials of hatred on our devoted heads; pin-prick of light stabbing the darkness, seeking the unwary and dashing them quick and sure into eternity. Ah, well, we were men then, not incompetent imbeciles, and the soothing nectar of good, honest toil filled our souls with contentment. Then the good, wholesome night, whiling away an hour or two of rest with Monsieur and Madam, skiting about our beloved Australia. Loving well and fighting well, lying well, but forgivable, for, parted from our land, it became a desirable Eden, and we painted vivid pictures to the open-mouthed. wondering peasants.

They are far away now, the old days. Flanders, the old farmhouse, the old French people, the old scenes. the white crosses, the impressions somewhat obliterated, we who fought forgot, but those who saw us fight remember.

Old Messieur with his gout and stick, the quaint old-world Madam, the bright-eyed French lass who loved the bold Diggars, and the kiddies - all in a cheering procession to pay the digger homage, saviours of Amiens, and good fellows, all competent enough to be trusted with their country's reputation, but incompetent enough for work. The little badge is in my lapel now, pride is unquenchable, and it will be my excuse for missing the finer points of commanding a billet.

OLD LETTERS

Written after reading some old letters returned from France

What tragedy lies on those written sheets,
What humour lies thereon;
What thoughts from every mood of mind,
What grief is penned upon;
What noble minds the thoughts came from,
As a mother wrote : "My noble son!"
What thoughts and hopes are penned in love.
Will we meet again? Pray God, anon.

THE LETTERS;

One is marked "Dead Letter Office,"
One "Somewhere in France;"
One is ciphered, "Killed or Wounded,"
Another "Killed in France."

Map within *How to See Paris, its environs and the Battlefields* Motor Tours offered by Thomas Cook & Son, Paris 1925.

APRES LA GUERRE

Cook's Tourist Bureau is already making final arrangements for tours to the European Battlefields.- Newspaper item.

Over all a peaceful quiet reigns, the afternoon sun is warm and bright; peace is over all. A scarlet cloak covers the torn and ragged country side. A faint breeze wafts to, us the delicious scent of jasmine and roses. We trudge along the road that leads to the eastern horizon. Little groups of French peasants are working among the long grass, digging up barbed wire and filling up the old trenches - landmarks that at times have been our refuge - at others -.

We go up to the old village. Here, all is life. The debris of the shattered houses has been cleared away; the carpenters are at work. The ancient old priest looks strangely out of place standing in the shadow of his church. It is a new church, and has just been painted. The big handsome stone building where the village folk were wont to worship is no more. A few well directed shells laid it low - the stone was used for protection in the dug-outs. We stroll across the fields. Here and there curious little mounds dot the landscape; the poppies and daisies hide their nakedness; the breeze disturbs them, they nod their sweet lullaby.

Scarlet poppies... Poppies for sleep. The big, gaunt trees along the roadside are bursting in bud; soon you will not be able to see their shattered limbs. Somewhere among the young leaves birds are twittering. This is surely God's acre... Peace be unto you; greater love hath no man.

Down the road a motor car approaches in a cloud of dust. It travels at a furious speed. The birds stop their twittering and fly away. Cook's Tourists! Lolling back among the cushions and smoking big cigars are several of the idle rich. As they pass me a woman's laugh rings out - mirthless, and with forced gaiety. Blue blood! - Aristocrats. The poppies give me their answer. Theirs is a silent vigil.

NOTES

These stories were originally privately printed in un-dated 32 page stapled booklets and sold door-to-door by Scanlon and many other ex-Servicemen:

The Land of Memory, Memories of Little Mamzelle, Meeting Susette, The Chateau of the Dead, Goodbye Susette, The Limehouse Parade, M'sieur Gibraud, Goodbye; all appeared in *Bon Jour Digger*

A War Baby, Little M'amselle, My French Bride, The Musical Bombardment, Apres La Guerre; all appeared in the rare first edition of *Much in Little*.

The Curse of the Brute and Ruminations; appeared in *Humoresque*.

The Game, Take Me-Give me, and Old Letters; appeared in *Recollections*.

A Shattered Romance appeared in *Triolette*.

Out on a Night Patrol appeared in *Remembrance*.

Madaemoiselle Longun appeared in *Old Memories*.

Tell Them This, A Tragedy of Love and War, The Unknown; appeared on *Bon Sonte*.

Nanette appeared in *The Vengeance of Etna*. It also appears as Wine, Women and Morals in *The Awful Australian*.

The image on page 114 is from *In a Nutshell*.